D1613019

RUSSELL SANDBERG

RELIGION AND MARRIAGE LAW

The Need for Reform

BRISTOL
UNIVERSITY
PRESS

First published in Great Britain in 2021 by

Bristol University Press
University of Bristol
1-9 Old Park Hill
Bristol
BS2 8BB
UK
t: +44 (0)117 954 5940
e: bup-info@bristol.ac.uk

Details of international sales and distribution partners are available at
bristoluniversitypress.co.uk

British Library Cataloguing in Publication Data
A catalogue record for this book is available from the British Library

ISBN 978-1-5292-1280-8 hardcover
ISBN 978-1-5292-1281-5 ePub
ISBN 978-1-5292-1282-2 ePdf

Cover design: blu inc, Bristol
Front cover image: frantic/Alamy Stock Photo 2B6M64P

To Emma, with love.

Contents

About the Author

Russell Sandberg is a Professor of Law at Cardiff University, UK. His research interrogates the interaction between Law and the Humanities. He is the author of *Law and Religion* (Cambridge University Press, 2011), the first textbook in the field; *Religion, Law and Society* (Cambridge University Press, 2014), which explores the interplay between the legal and sociological study of religion; and *Subversive Legal History: A Manifesto for the Future of Legal Education* (Routledge, 2021), which argues that history should be at the beating heart of the Law curriculum. He is editor or co-editor of seven edited collections and serves as the series editor of three book series published by Routledge (the ICLARS Series on Law and Religion, Transforming Legal Histories and Leading Works in Law) as well as the Anthem Studies in Law Reform.

The relationship between religion and family law has emerged as a particular focus of his work. He was co-investigator (with Professor Gillian Douglas, Professor Norman Doe, Professor Sophie Gilliat-Ray and Dr Asma Khan) of the first comparative empirical study of religious tribunals in England and Wales and their jurisdiction in relation to marriage and divorce, which was funded by the AHRC/ESRC Religion and Society programme. This led to a number of publications including the edited collection *Religion and Legal Pluralism* (Ashgate, 2015).

He is on Twitter (@sandbergrlaw) and has his own website and blog at: sandbergrlaw.wordpress.com.

Acknowledgements

The ideas and arguments in this book have been formulated over a number of years and have been rehearsed and corrected in a variety of forms and settings over the years from conference papers to blog posts, from taught seminars to academic articles, from Zoom meetings to discussions on social media. I am therefore indebted to a range of friends, colleagues, students and strangers for their indulgence and feedback. Particular thanks are also due to those who read the book in draft (Frank Cranmer, Dr Patrick Nash and Dr Sharon Thompson) and also to the staff at Bristol University Press, particularly Helen Davis, Freya Trand, Millie Prekop and the anonymous reviewers, for their enthusiasm for and professional commitment to the text. I owe the most, of course, to my family and especially to my partner, Emma, who have taught me how love abides in the face of everything.

ONE

Introduction: Marital Problems

The need for reform

This book argues that the law relating to marriage and the regulation of adult intimate relationships in England and Wales is in desperate need of reform. The number of marriages is falling. Office for National Statistics (ONS) data[1] shows that the marriage rate by 2017 (the number of marriages per 1,000 unmarried men and women aged 16 years and over) has decreased, by 75% for men and by 69% for women since 1972, to be the lowest on record (since 1862) and the number of marriages of opposite-sex couples has decreased by 45%. This decline is particularly pronounced in relation to religious marriages. While in 1900 religious ceremonies accounted for 85% of all marriages, and by the late 1970s were 49% of all marriages, by 2017 only 22% of all marriages were religious ceremonies, the lowest percentage on record, with civil

---

[1]   The statistics that follow are taken from a number of reports on the Office for National Statistics website: 'Marriages in England and Wales: 2017'; 'Marriage and Cohabitation (General Lifestyle Survey Overview – A Report on the 2011 General Lifestyle Survey)'; and 'Population Estimates by Marital Status and Living Arrangements, England and Wales: 2019'. They exclude the significant number of marriages that take place overseas.

marriages having outnumbered religious marriages every year since 1992.

By contrast, the number of cohabiting couples has risen sharply. ONS data shows that the proportion of non-married women aged 18 to 49 who were cohabiting increased from one in ten in 1979 to over a third in 2011. Of those living in a couple, 21.9% were now cohabiting, and among those aged 16 to 29 years this figure rose to 69.2%. Moreover, the 'common law marriage myth' remains prevalent, with a British Social Attitudes Survey conducted in 2018 showing that almost half those surveyed (46%) explicitly agreed with the incorrect statement that 'couples who live together for a period of time have a common law marriage which gives them the same rights as married couples'.[2] Moreover, this figure rose to 55% in relation to households with children.

Marriage law in England and Wales has failed to adapt to this changing social reality. Not only does it single out marriage and civil partnerships for protection, providing virtually no rights for cohabiting couples, but the law of opposite-sex marriage is also based on a distinction between marriages according to the rites of the Church of England (which in this context includes the Church in Wales) and all other marriages.

The law regulating marriage is a historical relic which reflects a bygone age of a Judaeo-Christian society. It is true that in the 21st century successive governments have made a series of progressive but ad hoc reforms, most notably the introduction of civil partnerships and same-sex marriage. However, these changes have been bolted on to a legal framework that is no longer fit for purpose. This has resulted in a law on marriage that is controversial, complex and often misunderstood.

---

[2] Anne Barlow, 'Modern Marriage Myths: The Dichotomy Between Expectations of Legal Rationality and Lived Lives', in Rajnaara C. Akhtar, Patrick Nash and Rebecca Probert (eds), *Cohabitation and Religious Marriage* (Bristol University Press, 2020) 39, 43–4.

This is especially the case in relation to religion. English and Welsh marriage law is inconsistent, unprincipled and discriminatory. It not only stipulates different rules for different religious groups but also excludes certain religious and non-religious practices. Religious marriages must take place in a registered building in order to be legally recognised, therefore excluding groups who either do not have such buildings or whose traditions involve marriage ceremonies elsewhere such as outside, in the home or at a community venue. Couples who enter into these so-called 'unregistered religious marriage' (that is, religious marriages that do not comply with the requirements of marriage law) are married religiously but not legally. As a result, they lack legal redress on relationship breakdown or the death of a partner and so need to resolve any disputes themselves or turn to religious tribunals such as Sharia councils. The couples are in the same legal position as cohabitants.

Reform of the law is needed because a number of wedding ceremonies currently take place outside the legal framework. Many of the couples who have such ceremonies consider themselves married at the end of it but they are married in the eyes of the law (and benefit from the legal rights that come with marriage) only once they undergo a further ceremony in the register office. This includes not only unregistered religious marriage but also ceremonies by non-religious bodies and celebrants: Humanists UK alone conducts around 1,000 ceremonies a year[3] and a recent study estimated that independent celebrants conduct 10,000 ceremonies a year in England and Wales,[4] but these ceremonies are also not currently legally

---

[3] All-Party Parliamentary Humanist Group, *'Any Lawful Impediment?' A Report of the All-Party Parliamentary Humanist Group's Inquiry into the Legal Recognition of Humanist Marriage in England and Wales* (2018) 9.

[4] Stephanie Pywell, 'The Day of their Dreams: Celebrant-Led Wedding Celebration Ceremonies' [2020] *Child and Family Law Quarterly* 177. This figure is an estimation based on responses received which assumes that those who did not respond are as active as those who did.

binding. This book argues that reform is needed primarily to deal with these two issues of unregistered religious marriages and non-religious marriages.

Several calls for reform have acted on the presumption that unregistered religious marriages are problematic per se. They have sought to ban all unregistered religious marriages by prohibiting religious ceremonies that occur before legal ceremonies and/or by penalising those who conduct them. This book does not agree with such an approach. Unregistered religious marriages can lead to discrimination, disadvantage and suffering – and there is a need for legal redress to be provided in such situations. However, this is not always the case.

There are various reasons why people enter into unregistered religious marriages. Some do so in order that they can date. It allows the couple to be together without being chaperoned. For such couples, a legally binding marriage would be inappropriate and premature. For others, however, the unregistered religious marriage may be the result of the strictness of current marriage laws, with couples unable to have the ceremony that manifests their beliefs under the legal restrictions, such that a separate legal ceremony is needed afterwards and, indeed, may never occur. For some, the unregistered religious marriage exists because of an unawareness that such a ceremony is not legally binding. And for others, there is pressure or coercion to only undergo an unregistered religious marriage ceremony.

Unregistered religious marriages are not a problem where they are entered into wittingly and voluntarily. Autonomous and freely informed adults should be free to voluntarily enter into any intimate relationships that they wish to. There is an argument that legal redress might need to be provided if that relationship changes over time in a way that causes a detriment to one of the parties: if one gives up work or goes part time so as to look after children or the other party, for instance. But other than that, if the unregistered religious marriage results from a free choice by both of the parties then that should be respected.

In this book it will therefore be argued that legal change is needed to reflect two points of principle. The first is that legal redress should be provided to those in unregistered religious marriages, but only where the failure to comply with registration requirements is unwitting or is not truly voluntary by one of the parties. The second is that non-religious ceremonies (such as those conducted by humanist organisations) and ceremonies conducted by independent celebrants should be legally binding.

This book

The purpose of this book is to galvanise the need for reform by providing an accessible guide to the law as it currently stands while also arguing the need for consolidation, modernisation and reform, explaining why this is needed and how this could be achieved. It seeks to complement works on the topic which are more academic in nature.[5] This book has three objectives: (1) to explain and demystify the law, (2) to document and critically analyse the debate so far and (3) to suggest solutions, drawing upon and developing further the recent work of the Law Commission in relation to weddings law. It falls into three parts:

The first part, 'The Legal Framework', will elucidate the current position on how adult intimate relationships are governed by the law of England and Wales, with particular reference to how it affects religion. Chapter Two will explore the legal regulation of opposite-sex marriage, while Chapter Three will examine same-sex marriage, with discussion also of the law on civil partnerships.

---

[5] Such as the essays in Rajnaara C. Akhtar, Patrick Nash and Rebecca Probert (eds), *Cohabitation and Religious Marriage* (Bristol University Press, 2020).

The second part, 'The Road to Reform', will document the public debate so far on the need for reform, with particular reference to the two issues highlighted earlier. Chapter Five will explore the debate on unregistered religious marriages, while Chapter Six will look at non-religious marriages. Both of these issues have recently led to litigation and both of these chapters will conclude with a look at those respective cases and how they point to the need for reform.[6] Chapter Seven will then turn in detail to the radical reforms suggested by the Law Commission's consultation paper which would transform the law on how people get married but which would provide only limited mitigation to the problem of unregistered religious marriages.[7]

The final part, 'Reform Proposals', draws upon the previous chapters to propose specific reform proposals resting on the two points of principle outlined earlier. A package of reforms will be presented together with draft extracts of possible legislation that could enact such changes.

The statistics cited at the start of this chapter show that adult intimate relationships take different forms in the 21st century, meaning that laws enacted in the middle of the 20th century are no longer fit for purpose. This book provides an accessible guide to the current labyrinth of marriage law and a blueprint for much-needed reform.

---

[6]   *R (on Application of Harrison) v Secretary of State for Justice* [2020] EWHC 2096 (Admin); *Her Majesty's Attorney General v Akhter* [2020] EWCA Civ 122.

[7]   Law Commission, *Getting Married: A Consultation Paper on Weddings Law* (Consultation Paper 247, 2020).

PART I

The Legal Framework

TWO

Religion and Opposite-Sex Marriage

Introduction

This chapter begins our discussion of the current position on how adult intimate relationships are governed by the law of England and Wales, with particular reference to how it affects religion. It examines the legal regulation of opposite-sex marriage, placing the current law as found in the Marriage Act 1949 within its historical context to explore why the Church of England has been placed in a special legal position and why the current position of other religious weddings is often mis-understood. Given these misunderstandings, this chapter will begin with a discussion of the current law before placing this within its historical context.

The current law

Religious groups may conduct marriage ceremonies, but for a marriage conducted in England and Wales to be legally binding it needs to comply with the requirements laid out in marriage law.[1]

---

[1]   There are also rules whereby marriages conducted in other jurisdictions are considered to be legally binding in England and Wales. This book does not focus on these but all references to legally binding marriages or marriages conducted under the Marriage Act 1949 also includes such marriages.

The Marriage Act 1949 differentiates between marriages solemnised according to the rites of the Church of England/Church in Wales and marriages otherwise solemnised. This second category of marriages otherwise solemnised includes: (1) civil marriages in a register office or in approved premises; (2) marriages 'according to the usages of the Society of Friends'; (3) marriages 'between a man and a woman professing the Jewish religion according to the usages of the Jews'; and (4) marriages in any place of worship registered under the Places of Worship Registration Act 1855 and section 41 of the Marriage Act 1949.

All religions (other than the three specifically named in the Act: the Church of England/Church in Wales, Society of Friends and Jews) fall under this last category. They can therefore conduct lawful marriages provided that their buildings are registered and there is a registrar or authorised person present. Under section 43 of the Marriage Act 1949, an authorised person (such as the minister) can be appointed by the governing body or trustees of the building provided that their details are then authorised to the Registrar General and to the Superintendent Registrar of the registration district in which the building is situated.

The fact that three religious groups are specifically named in the legislation has led to some confusion.[2] A Council of Europe resolution and some commentators have asserted that only the named faiths have to register their marriages.[3] This is not true.

---

[2] Law Commission, *Getting Married: A Consultation Paper on Weddings Law* (Consultation Paper 247, 2020) para 5.25 et seq.

[3] Parliamentary Assembly of the Council of Europe Resolution 2253: *Sharia, the Cairo Declaration and the European Convention on Human Rights*, para 14.2; Aina Khan, 'Dilemmas Facing Muslims in the United Kingdom', in Susan Rutten, Benedicta Deogratias and Pauline Kruiniger (eds), *Martial Captivity* (Eleven Publishing, 2019) 309, 324; Siddique Patel, 'The Register our Marriage Campaign is Pioneering for Equality for Unregistered Marriage', The Law Society blog (17 September 2019).

There is no gap in the Marriage Act 1949 for religious groups other than the three mentioned. The problem is not that other religious marriages cannot be legally recognised under the Act. It is, rather, that the requirements required for such recognition indirectly discriminate against some religions: the requirements that the wedding must be inside a registered place of worship and that a prescribed choice of words must be used do not fit with some religious traditions.

This has led to some religious marriages in those traditions not complying with the requirements of the Marriage Act 1949: the problem of unregistered religious marriages. Although the parties often see themselves as being married and are married in the eyes of their faith, their marriages are not legally recognised and therefore do not provide rights and relief to the parties in the case of relationship breakdown. They are legally cohabitants rather than spouses.

By contrast to religious marriages, there is a gap in the Marriage Act in relation to non-religious marriages, such as those conducted by belief organisations and independent celebrants. Under marriage law there is a firm distinction between religious and civil marriage. Civil weddings must be solemnised in the presence of the Superintendent Registrar and Registrar. There is no option of having an authorised person from a non-religious organisation. No religious service can be used in civil ceremonies and a building with a recent or continuing religious connection cannot be an 'approved premises'.[4] This means that ceremonies solely conducted by belief organisations and independent celebrants are outside current marriage law.

Under the current law different rules exist for the various different ways in which marriages are solemnised. This adds significantly to the complexity and inaccessibility of the law.

---

[4] Marriage Act 1949, s45A(4); Marriages and Civil Partnerships (Approved Premises) Regulations 2005/3168, Schedule 1.

This is not helped by the fact that the distinctions drawn in the law are the result of historical quirks rather than matters of principle. Moreover, throughout its history marriage law has been moulded by Christian hands. These fingerprints can still be found in the current law, which sees Christian marriage (or more particularly Church of England marriage) as the norm.

The remainder of this chapter will seek to contextualise the current law by providing a brief historical account of how opposite-sex marriage law has developed. This will uncover and explain the Christian influence upon the law and the special legal position of the Church of England. The distinctions drawn in the law as it stands arise from historical circumstances and no longer serve any useful purpose in the 21st century but, rather, confuse and exclude in ways that underline the need for reform.

The Christian origins of marriage law

Some caution is required when talking about the Christian origins of and influence upon marriage law. As Julian Rivers has warned, some references to Christianity by law-makers and adjudicators can be dismissed 'as mere rhetorical flourishes'.[5] Moreover, the Christian church has not been the sole influencer upon the law, as Don Browning has observed:

> Christianity has had an enormous influence on Western family law but it has not had this influence all by itself. It is best to think of Christian marriage and family theories as special twists brought to a variety of other folk, philosophical, legal, and economic perspectives on marriage and the family. Christian marriage and family traditions

---

[5] Julian Rivers, 'Is English Law Christian?', in Nick Spencer (ed), *Religion and Law* (Theos, 2012) 143.

have mixed with influences from Judaism, Greek philosophy, Roman law and Germanic law.[6]

Yet, in the context of England, marriage provides an example of a social relationship which was formerly exclusively recognised and regulated by the Church.[7] From the mid–12th century, the church courts had exclusive jurisdiction over marriage and divorce, applying Roman Catholic canon law. This continued following the Reformation of the 16th century, when the Roman Catholic Church with its authority in Rome was ousted and replaced with the Anglican Church of England. As Geoffrey Elton has commented, England 'wore her Reformation with a difference':[8] the divorce from Rome in the 1530s under Henry VIII was not a religious upheaval that required political and constitutional reconstruction, it was a political and constitutional act that led in time to religious upheaval.

This meant that the radical reform of marriage which occurred on the Continent was not replicated in England: the existing canon law of the Church continued to apply until it was replaced unless it was 'contrariant or repugnant to the King's prerogative royal, or the customs, laws and statutes of this realm'.[9] What did change was the legal status (and later the religious persuasion) of the English Church: a flurry of Reformation statutes saw the king become recognised as 'the

---

[6] Don S. Browning, 'Family Law and Christian Jurisprudence', in John Witte Jr and Frank S. Alexander, *Christianity and Law* (Cambridge University Press, 2008) 163.

[7] For general discussion of the legal framework affecting religious groups and its history see Russell Sandberg, *Law and Religion* (Cambridge University Press, 2011) chapters 2 and 4.

[8] Geoffrey R. Elton, 'The Reformation in England', in Geoffrey R. Elton (ed), *The New Cambridge Modern History Volume 2: The Reformation, 1520–1559* (2nd edition, Cambridge University Press, 1990) 262.

[9] Submission of the Clergy Act 1533.

only supreme head in earth of the Church of England'.[10] And this meant that other forms of religion were now not only illegal but treasonous.

Although there were some minor amendments, chiefly through the enactment of the Canons Ecclesiastical 1603–4, it was Marriage Act 1753 that provided the watershed moment. This Act provided the foundations of the modern law on marriage. It imposed the canon law requirements upon all weddings except for Jews and Quakers: all marriages were to take the form of a public ceremony in the parish church at which a clergyman would officiate according to authorised rites, and it required that the marriage be preceded by banns or licence. Breach of any of these requirements, which had previously made a marriage irregular, would now render it void.

Although it was not the first attempt to regularise the performance and registration of marriage, the Marriage Act 1753 is often regarded to be a pivotal moment providing certainty as to who was married and stopping marriages taking place in ways that the State was unaware of. This was problematic because marital status bestowed certain legal rights, and social attitudes at the time saw children born out of wedlock as being illegitimate. Although it has now been questioned whether the Act largely reinforced existing social conventions rather than stamping out a serious and prevalent problem of marriages being conducted in various and unusual ways,[11] nevertheless, the effect of the legislation was clear. The emphasis upon marriage taking place in public continues to underscore the current law. The Act imposed uniformity: everyone had to marry according to the rites of the Church of England except Quakers and Jews, to whom the Act did not apply but whose weddings were subsequently held to be valid by the courts. In

---

[10] Act of Supremacy 1534.

[11] Rebecca Probert, *Marriage Law and Practice in the Long Eighteenth Century* (Cambridge University Press, 2009).

this respect, the 1753 Act represented a significant shift away from marriage being exclusively regulated by the Church in that now, common law courts could determine whether the Act had been breached.

It was not until the Marriage Act 1836, some 80 years later, that provision was made for 'civil marriage', permitting marriages to take place in register offices, following a completely civil ceremony in the presence of a Registrar and witnesses. That Act also provided that buildings registered as a place of religious worship could be registered for solemnising marriages therein. This was a key component of the piecemeal toleration of other forms of religion. The foundations of the modern law of marriage were now fully laid out. The law had been built around the historic framework of Church of England weddings without any thought of principle.

The legal requirement in the 1753 Act that marriages were to occur in the parish church has been understood as creating a legal right for parishioners – and nowadays those with a qualifying connection –[12] to marry in the Church of England parish church,[13] with Church of England clergy being afforded conscience clauses to refuse to solemnise marriages of parishioners in certain circumstances such as where the former spouse is still living.[14] Even when the Matrimonial Causes Act 1857 transferred jurisdiction over matrimonial causes from the church courts of the Church of England to the common law courts, section 22 of the Act stipulated that the common law courts should continue to apply the same principles as the church courts had done. So entrenched and interlinked were the law of the Church and the law of the State regarding marriage that when the Church of England was disestablished in Wales in

---

[12] Church of England Marriage Measure 2008. Similar provision has been made in relation to the Church in Wales: Marriage (Wales) Act 2010.

[13] Cf Norman Doe, *The Legal Framework of the Church of England: A Critical Study in a Comparative Context* (Clarendon Press, 1996), 359–60.

[14] Matrimonial Causes Act 1965 s8(2).

1920,[15] provision was made that this would not affect marriage law and that in relation to marriage law the term Church of England would still be understood to include reference to the Church in Wales.[16]

It is true that differences between Church law and State law on marriage have increased. Most notably, although the prohibited degrees of consanguinity (prohibited relationships by blood) and affinity (prohibited relationships by marriage) have a clear religious base, a divergence has arisen between those of the Church and those of the State, leading to the enactment of a conscience clause permitting clergy to refuse to solemnise the marriage of those whose marriage would have been void before the State law changed.[17] Therefore, as Julian Rivers has commented, the law on marriage remains 'compatible with a recognisably Christian view', with the Church remaining 'free to teach a higher ideal, to which Christians and others can aspire'.[18] The fact that such differences of opinion have been minimised by the use of conscience clauses underscores the basic agreement between Church and State regarding many of the definitional attributes of marriage and how modern marriage law continues to be shaped by and interlinked with Christianity.

This can be underlined by contrasting the law on marriage with the law on divorce. The law on divorce, found in the Matrimonial Causes Act 1973, is completely secular. English law provides no recognition of 'religious divorces', a divorce affected exclusively under religious law has no effect recognised by State law. However, in recent years English law has also taken

---

[15] Welsh Church Act 1914.
[16] Welsh Church (Temporalities) Act 1919 s6; Marriage Act s78(2).
[17] Marriage Act 1949, s5A (amended by the Marriage (Prohibited Degrees of Relationship) Act 1986, s3); Marriage Act 1949 (Remedial) Order 2006.
[18] Julian Rivers, 'Is English Law Christian?', in Nick Spencer (ed), *Religion and Law* (Theos, 2012) 143, 149.

on a limited facilitative role in that the Divorce (Religious Marriages) Act 2002 (now contained in section 10A of the Matrimonial Causes Act 1973) provides that a court may delay the making absolute of a divorce decree until the parties have certified that a religious divorce has been granted by the appropriate authorities. The provision means that one of the parties cannot refuse a religious divorce if they wish to get divorced under State law. This was passed to stop the problem of the 'chained wife', whom the husband was content to divorce under State law but who remained married in the eyes of her faith.[19] At present, only the Jewish religion is included within this provision but it is open to other religions to seek to be 'prescribed' within the legislation. The secular starting point and equal playing field found in relation to divorce contrasts with that in relation to marriage.

Conclusion

This chapter has shown that the legal framework found in the Marriage Act 1949 consolidates a law on marriage which is significantly older. As John Eekelaar has noted, marriage law does not have 'a dishonourable history': 'marriage law, confused though it is, has developed by making a series of accommodations with various groups and points of view'.[20] It is not only the case that historically marriage has been moulded by Christian hands; it is also true that the whole legal framework is built upon that historic Church of England law of marriage. The distinctions that underpin the Marriage Act

---

[19] This has sometimes been referred to as 'marital captivity', that is: 'A situation wherein someone is unable to terminate his or her religious marriage, i.e. keeping a spouse "trapped" in a marriage against his or her will': Susan Rutten and Benedicta Deogratias, 'Introduction', in Susan Rutten, Benedicta Deogratias and Pauline Kruiniger (eds), *Martial Captivity* (Eleven Publishing, 2019) 1, 9.

[20] John Eekelaar, 'Marriage: A Modest Proposal' [2013] *Family Law* 83.

1949 arise from historical quirk, and the fact that different rules then apply to different forms of marriage would on its own be reason enough for reform. This has resulted in an antiquated and overly complex legal framework that indirectly discriminates against some religious traditions and excludes non-religious beliefs. Yet, English law remains wedded to this historical legal framework. Any reforms that are made continue to be ad hoc accommodations. This will be explored in the next chapter, which will document how the recognition and regulation of same-sex relationships has been achieved in recent years by seeking to protect and replicate the legal framework discussed in this chapter.

THREE

Religion and Same-Sex Marriage

Introduction

For a legal status which has existed for less than 20 years, the law concerning same-sex partnerships and religion has had a turbulent and somewhat confusing history. This chapter examines the story so far. The first part examines how the Civil Partnership Act 2004 originally ignored religion, copying the template of civil marriage. It then charts how this approach fell apart with the introduction of religious civil partnerships. The second part looks at the Marriage (Same Sex Couples) Act 2013 that built upon the existing structure for opposite-sex marriage rather than using the opportunity to craft a modernised, rationalised and codified law on marriage. This has led to an increasingly complex legal framework as shown by the 'quadruple lock' that permits but does not oblige religious groups to conduct same-sex marriages.

Civil partnerships

The Civil Partnership Act 2004 was introduced in response to two private Member's bills, which interestingly both sought to introduce a mechanism for both homo- and heterosexual couples.[1]

---

[1] Stephen Cretney, *Same Sex Relationships: From Odious Crime to 'Gay Marriage'* (Oxford University Press, 2006) 16.

However, unlike these Bills, the Civil Partnership Act 2004 provided recognition and protection only in the case of 'a relationship between two people of the same sex' (section 1(1)). Much of the Civil Partnership Act 2004 used 'civil marriage as a template for the processes, rights and responsibilities that go with civil partnership'.[2] The restrictions on who could enter a civil partnership replicated those for marriage, but for the requirement that the partners had to be of the same sex (sections 3 and 4). Using the template of civil marriage meant that significant confusion existed as to the differences between the two statuses. In *Wilkinson v Kitzinger*[3] it was stated that the Act bestowed upon civil partners 'effectively all the rights, responsibilities, benefits and advantages of civil marriage save the name'.

The use of the template of civil marriage also meant that, originally, civil partnerships lived up to their name and were civil and not religious. In the same way as a religious service could not be used during a civil marriage ceremony, originally under section 6 of the Civil Partnership Act 2004 a religious service could not be used 'while the civil partnership registrar is officiating at the signing', and the place at which two people could register as civil partners could not be in 'religious premises'. A distinction therefore existed between marriage, which could be civil or religious, and civil partnerships, which could only be civil.

This distinction neatly defused opposition from some traditional Christian churches.[4] Religious organisations could not conduct civil partnerships themselves. They could hold services to mark such unions following civil partnership ceremonies but without any legal affect. This firm line provided clarity,

---

[2] Jacqui Smith, House of Commons Hansard, 12 October 2004, col 174.
[3] [2006] EWHC (Fam) 2022 at para 121.
[4] See Stephen Cretney, *Same Sex Relationships: From Odious Crime to 'Gay Marriage'* (Oxford University Press, 2006) 25.

but the exclusion of religions from this new rite of passage proved controversial.

The desire of some religious groups to conduct and register civil partnerships eventually led to amendments being tabled to what was to become section 202 of the Equality Act 2010.[5] This amended section 6 of the Civil Partnership Act 2004, which, together with the eventual resulting Regulations,[6] removed the ban on civil partnerships taking place on religious premises. However, a religious service is still prohibited 'while the civil partnership registrar is officiating at the signing' (s2(5)). The right of religious groups to choose not to conduct civil partnerships was guaranteed by a new section inserted into the Civil Partnership Act 2004 stating that: 'For the avoidance of doubt, nothing in this Act places an obligation on religious organisations to host civil partnerships if they do not wish to'. However, by contrast, no protection was afforded to registrars or relationship counsellors who felt that the law on civil partnerships was incompatible with their religious beliefs, and the courts held that this did not amount to religious discrimination,[7] a stance later upheld by the European Court of Human Rights.[8]

The introduction of religious civil partnerships disregarded the template of civil marriage and meant that, despite their name, civil partnerships were no longer necessarily civil. This move did not, however, create complete parity between opposite-sex and same-sex couples. Now, in the same way that opposite-sex couples had a choice between a religious and civil

---

5   For example, see Frank Cranmer, 'Quakers and the Campaign for Same-Sex Marriage', in Russell Sandberg (ed), *Religion and Legal Pluralism* (Ashgate, 2015) 67.

6   Marriages and Civil Partnerships (Approved Premises) (Amendment) Regulations 2011.

7   *Ladele v London Borough of Islington* [2009] EWCA (Civ) 1357; *McFarlane v Relate Avon Ltd* [2010] EWCA (Civ) 880.

8   *Eweida and Others v United Kingdom* (2013) 57 EHRR 8.

marriage, same-sex couples had a choice between a religious and 'civil' civil partnership. However, same-sex couples could not enter into marriages and opposite-sex couples could not enter into civil partnerships.

Same-sex marriages

In September 2011, the Home Office announced a public consultation to consider how to make civil marriage available to same-sex couples. This focus on civil and not religious marriage was intended to mirror the original distinction made at the time of the Civil Partnership Act 2004. The 2012 consultation covered 'civil marriage for same-sex couples only – not religious marriage or opposite-sex civil partnerships'. The consultation included a question, however, which asked whether respondents agreed or disagreed with the government's proposal not to open up religious marriage to same-sex couples. The government's response to the consultation later that year revealed that the majority of the respondents who directly answered this question disagreed with the proposal and wanted religious marriage ceremonies to be available to same-sex couples.[9] Those quoted in favour of same-sex religious marriage, which included campaign groups such as Stonewall and Liberty and a number of religious organisations, typically saw this as a question of religious freedom. Those who disagreed with same-sex religious marriage, such as the Church of England and the Muslim Council of Britain, expressed concern that they would be pressured or forced to conduct such ceremonies either under domestic law or following a ruling of the European Court of Human Rights.

The government's response was to accept the argument that 'religious organisations should be permitted to conduct such

---

[9] HM Government, *Equal Marriage: The Government's Response* (December 2012) 16.

ceremonies if they wish to' but that it would remain 'unlawful for a religious organisation to marry same-sex couples unless it expressly consents and opts in according to a formal process put in place by legislation'. The government proposed a 'quadruple lock' providing four statutory provisions which would protect those religious organisations which did not wish to marry same-sex couples. The first 'lock' would be an explicit statement that no religious organisation or individual minister can be compelled to marry same-sex couples or to permit this to happen on their premises. The second 'lock' would make it unlawful for religious organisations or their ministers to marry same-sex couples unless they have expressly opted in to do so. The third 'lock' would amend the Equality Act 2010 to state that no discrimination claim could be brought against religious organisations or individual members for refusing to marry a same-sex couple or allowing their premises to be used for this purpose. The fourth 'lock' would state that the legislation did not apply to the Church of England and the Church in Wales, meaning that it would continue to be illegal for those churches to marry same-sex couples or to opt-in to do so without explicit further legislation.

This was an 'everything but the kitchen sink' approach designed to offer protection so that any religious organisation that did not wish to conduct same-sex marriages would not fall foul of domestic law. The 'locks' were also felt necessary, given the complex law on marriage and how it deals differently with different religions. According to the government's response, the fourth 'lock' recognised the 'unique position of the Church of England as the Established Church' and ensured that 'the legislation does not interfere with the Canon Law understanding of marriage … which we accept will be narrower than that of the civil law'.[10]

---

[10] Ibid 18.

The Marriage (Same Sex Couples) Act 2013 largely followed the conclusions reached in the government's response to the consultation. All parts of the 'quadruple lock' were present but, confusingly, were dispersed throughout the legislation. The Act made the marriage of same-sex couples lawful, creating an opt-in system for religious same-sex marriages which applied to all religious organisations other than the Church of England and Church in Wales (sections 3, 4 and 5). This opt-in was to be exercised by the religious organisation, not the couple getting married. The Act further stated that no person or religious organisation is to be compelled to undertake an opt-in activity or to conduct, consent to, be present at, carry out, or otherwise participate in a same-sex marriage where the reason for not doing that is that the relevant marriage concerns a same-sex couple (s2).

The Equality Act 2010 was amended in two notable respects. First, the rule in section 110 (that states that an employee will remain personally liable for unlawful acts committed in the course of employment where the employer is also liable) was amended so that it does not apply in relation to refusing to conduct, consent to, be present at, carry out, or otherwise participate in a same-sex marriage where the reason for not doing so is that the relevant marriage concerns a same-sex couple. Second, a new Part 6A was added to Schedule 3 to provide that it is not discrimination in relation to goods and service where a person does not conduct, consent to, be present at, carry out, or otherwise participate in a same-sex marriage where the reason for not doing so is that the relevant marriage concerns a same-sex couple.

In addition to providing that the Church of England cannot opt in to solemnise same-sex marriages, the Marriage (Same Sex Couples) Act 2013 provides special protection for the law and practice of the Established Church to continue to follow the previous understanding of marriage as being between members of the opposite-sex. Section 11 provides that 'in the law of England and Wales, marriage has the same effect in relation to same-sex couples as it has in relation to opposite-sex couples' and this applies to all 'legislation whenever passed or made'. However this does not apply to laws made by the Church of England or other ecclesiastical law. It is also stated that: 'Any duty of a member of the clergy to solemnize marriages (and any corresponding right of persons to have their marriages solemnized by members of the clergy) is not extended by this Act to marriages of same-sex couples' (s1(4)).

These provisions are necessary in part because the Marriage (Same Sex Couples) Act 2013 continues to bolt its changes upon the legal framework of the Marriage Act 1949, which focuses on registered places of religious worship. Rebecca Probert has noted that if the law instead changed to focusing on authorised persons, then same-sex couples could be married in accordance with religious rites without requiring religious organisations collectively to opt in.[11] This is reflected in the law on same-sex couples as a whole. Its complexity is the result not so much of the need to protect religious freedom but due to the need to do so within the outmoded framework erected for opposite-sex marriage. At all stages provisions have been bolted upon the current law, with the law on opposite-sex marriage often used as a template for reform. This is reflected further in the recent expansion of civil partnerships to opposite-sex couples. Following the Supreme Court's decision in *Steinfeld*[12] that the prohibition of opposite-sex civil partnership was incompatible with the European Convention on Human Rights, the government supported a private Member's bill, which became the Civil Partnerships, Marriages and Deaths (Registration etc) Act

---

[11] Rebecca Probert, 'A Uniform Marriage Law for England and Wales?' (2018) 30 (3) *Child and Family Law Quarterly* 259.

[12] *R (on the application of Steinfeld and Keidan) v Secretary of State for International Development* [2018] UKSC 32.

2019. This required the Secretary of State to make regulations extending civil partnerships to opposite-sex couples. Part 3 of the Civil Partnerships (Opposite-sex Couples) Regulations 2019 introduced a number of amendments providing further religious protections that have added yet a further degree of complexity to the law on intimate adult relationships.

This complexity would be bad enough, but it is also true that this focus on opposite-sex civil partnerships has left unsolved a much more statistically relevant issue: the fact that legal protection continues not to be afforded to cohabiting opposite-sex couples – who make up a significant chunk of the population.[13] It is difficult to disagree with Anne Barlow, who has argued that, although opposite-sex civil partnerships 'have been presented as the solution for cohabiting couples, implicitly rendering redundant the need for further cohabitation law reform', this change will be 'a remedy for the few not the many'.[14] Her work suggested that there are four overlapping groups of cohabitants and that these also apply to those in unregistered religious marriages: 'Ideologues' who reject legal marriage, 'Romantics' who simply believe in the relationship, 'Pragmatists' who are unaware of their situation but who marry or enter into a civil partnership once they become aware, and 'Uneven Couples' where one party is aware and the other is in ignorance and power is not evenly spread.[15] She concluded that opposite-sex civil partnerships will provide a vehicle only 'for couples who are both ideologically opposed to marriage

---

[13] See generally Jo Miles and Rebecca Probert, 'Civil Partnership: Ties that (Also) Bind' (2019) 31 (4) *Child and Family Law Quarterly* 303.

[14] Anne Barlow, 'Modern Marriage Myths: The Dichotomy Between Expectations of Legal Rationality and Lived Lives', in Rajnaara C. Akhtar, Patrick Nash and Rebecca Probert (eds), *Cohabitation and Religious Marriage* (Bristol University Press, 2020) 39, 40, 50.

[15] Ibid 49, drawing on Anne Barlow and Jayne Smithson, 'Legal Assumptions, Cohabitants' Talk and the Rocky Road to Reform' (2010) 22 (3) *Child and Family Law Quarterly* 328, 335–42.

and are legally aware'.[16] The ever-increasing complexities and inconsistencies of the current law and the fact that it continues to exclude a significant number of adult relationships raises the question of whether it is time to reform, consolidate and modernise the law.

Conclusion

This chapter has described the speedy development of a welcome but bewilderingly complex legal framework recognising and regulating same-sex relationships. The significant changes to the legal framework on same-sex relationships within a short time-scale reflect not only the changing social attitude towards homosexuality but also the limits of the pragmatic, ad hoc legislation that has been passed. An opportunity to return to the drawing board to develop a 21st-century law relating to adult intimate relationships has been lost. Instead, changes have been bolted on to the existing legal framework in a way that means that the law on adult intimate relationships is increasingly complex and continues to focus solely on particular relationship forms. This, added to the criticisms made in the last chapter about the indirect discrimination against some religious traditions under the Marriage Act 1949, the exclusion of non-religious belief ceremonies and the way in which marriage law continues to be shaped by its Christian past, points to the need for reform. The next part will develop this further by focusing on two particular issues of concern that have been raised in recent years that further show the need for specific reform: unregistered religious marriages and non-religious marriages.

---

[16] Anne Barlow, 'Modern Marriage Myths: The Dichotomy Between Expectations of Legal Rationality and Lived Lives', in Rajnaara C. Akhtar, Patrick Nash and Rebecca Probert (eds), *Cohabitation and Religious Marriage* (Bristol University Press, 2020) 39–50.

PART II

The Road to Reform

FOUR

Unregistered Religious Marriages

Introduction

This chapter explores the debate on unregistered religious marriages. It will fall into three sections. The first part will outline how the unregistered religious marriage issue has arisen in public debate, looking at the empirical studies that highlighted the issue and the numerous reviews that have taken place which have highlighted it as a problem and sought to solve it. The second part will then examine and critique a particular reform proposal that has come to the fore: a new criminal offence penalising celebrants. The chapter will conclude with discussion of a high-profile case – the Family Court and Court of Appeal decisions in *Akhter v Khan*[1] – which highlighted the problem of unregistered religious marriages and the lack of legal relief for those in such marriages and the need for legislative rather than judicial reform.

The fear of Sharia

While public debate about the accommodation of minority religious cultures is long standing, the current impetus for

---

[1] *Akhter v Khan* [2018] EWFC 54; *Her Majesty's Attorney General v Akhter* [2020] EWCA Civ 122.

reform can be dated back to a lecture by the then Archbishop of Canterbury, Rowan Williams, at the Royal Courts of Justice in 2008.[2] Williams' lecture was not about marriage law but, rather, about the general accommodation of religious law by State law and, in particular, the operation of religious tribunals. In his lecture, Williams raised the question of 'what it is like to live under more than one (legal) jurisdiction' and how (and how far) the civil law of the land should recognise or accommodate a legal pluralism based on religious adherence. He suggested that 'we have to think a little harder about the role and rule of law in a plural society of overlapping identities'. This caused uproar: a succession of senior figures came out to condemn Williams' thinking, while the television news graphically illustrated the item with footage of stonings.[3]

However, the heat of the immediate media and political coverage gave way over time to light, thanks to a number of academic studies.[4] The debate came to focus on the role that Sharia law played in the lives of Muslims in England and Wales and what the role of the State should be in ensuring that adherence to the authority of religious groups did not result in discrimination and disadvantage. Academics came to characterise this as the 'minorities within minorities' issue: the concern that deference to the religious group may reduce the rights and obligations that a member of the group would ordinarily enjoy by virtue of their citizenship of the State, particularly where the polity of the group differs from that of the State as regards gender roles.[5] A number of empirical studies were conducted that revealed how particular

---

[2] Rowan Williams, 'Civil and Religious Law in England: A Religious Perspective' (2008) 10 *Ecclesiastical Law Journal* 262.

[3] See Ralph Grillo, *Muslim Families, Politics and the Law* (Ashgate, 2015).

[4] See Norman Doe, *Comparative Religious Law* (Cambridge University Press, 2018); Rossella Bottoni and Silvio Ferrari (eds), *Routledge Handbook of Religious Laws* (Routledge, 2019); and Burkhard Josef Berkmann, *The Internal Law of Religions* (Routledge, 2020).

[5] See Ayelet Shachar, *Multicultural Jurisdictions: Cultural Differences and Women's Rights* (Cambridge University Press, 2001).

religious tribunals, especially Sharia councils, operate.[6] These studies focused inevitably on the most 'mainstream' councils, those who are most willing to engage with academics and have experience doing so. With the exception of the courts of the Church of England, religious-based approaches to adjudication are not part of the State court system in England and Wales. They are instead formed by religious groups and are variously styled according to the needs of the faith community in question, with ranging degrees of formality. It is simply unknown how many religious-based forms of adjudication exist in general, or how many Sharia councils operate in particular. Nothing is known about the more informal tribunals, since the empirical work that has taken place has focused on particular institutions and we have no reason to think that these are representative. With the exception of the Sharia Councils studied and the *batei din* within the Jewish community, we know very little about how non-Christian religions, ethnic and cultural groups resolve their disputes.[7]

The empirical studies conducted did, however, highlight the problem of unregistered religious marriages.[8] For instance, the Social Cohesion and Civil Law project conducted at Cardiff

---

[6] Empirical studies have included Sonia Shah-Kazemi, *Untying the Knot: Muslim Women, Divorce and the Shariah* (Nuffield Foundation, 2001); Samia Bano, *Muslim Women and Shari'ah Councils* (Palgrave, 2012); and the 'Social Cohesion and Civil Law: Marriage, Divorce and Religious Courts' Research Project at Cardiff University: Gillian Douglas, Norman Doe, Sophie Gilliat-Ray, Russell Sandberg and Asma Khan, *Social Cohesion and Civil Law: Marriage, Divorce and Religious Courts* (Cardiff, 2011).

[7] Amina Hussain, 'Legal Pluralism, Religious Conservatism', in Russell Sandberg (ed), *Religion and Legal Pluralism* (Ashgate, 2015) 151.

[8] This has become the focus of a vast literature. See, for example, Kathryn O'Sullivan and Leyla Jackson, 'Muslim Marriage (Non) Recognition: Implications and Possible Solutions' (2017) 39 (1) *Journal of Social Welfare and Family Law* 22; Rebecca Probert and Shabana Saleem, 'The Legal Treatment of Islamic Marriage Ceremonies' (2018) 7 (3) *Oxford Journal of Law and Religion* 376; and the essays in Rajnaara C. Akhtar, Patrick Nash and Rebecca Probert (eds), *Cohabitation and Religious Marriage* (Bristol University Press, 2020).

University found that over half of the cases dealt with by the Sharia Council in the study involved couples who did not have legally binding marriages. The research expressed concern that such litigants had very limited remedies under English civil law on relationship breakdown and that they often did not realise that this was the case: they assumed that their religious marriage had legal effect under State law. It also pointed out that while those who had legally binding marriages had a choice of remedies on relationship breakdown in that they could use State law or the Sharia Council, those in unregistered religious marriages either had to resolve the issues themselves or use the Sharia Council. This lack of choice is problematic, given that other commentators have pointed to discrimination on grounds of gender that occurs within religious tribunals. This can take the form of resolving the dispute, but in ways that are unfair, or refusing the termination of the religious marriage at all, or at least placing obstacles in front of its dissolution.

The Cardiff research called for greater awareness and education concerning the requirements of marriage law, explaining the procedural requirements for a civil law marriage and the rights that are accrued as a result of marriage. However, in recent years a number of official reports have looked into the issue and have made suggestions for law reform.

The Law Commission

In 2015 the Law Commission carried out a scoping review into the law on getting married that indicated 'both a need and a desire for reform' of the law on marriage generally and stated that the 'perceived rise in religious–only marriages' was a reason for this.[9] It noted that although 'the precise number of

---

[9]   Law Commission, *Getting Married: A Scoping Paper* (2015) paras 1.36 and 1.33.

religious-only marriages is unknown, since by definition they do not appear in any state record', nevertheless 'it was telling that only 200 legal marriages in Muslim places of worship were recorded in 2010, against a backdrop population of 2,706,066 Muslims in the 2011 census' (para 1.35). Although the Law Commission saw reform as urgent, the government dragged its feet, commissioning a full review from the Law Commission only in June 2019. Their consultation paper outlining their proposals for reform was published in September 2020 and is discussed in detail in Chapter Six.

The Commission on Religion and Belief in British Public Life

The report of the Commission on Religion and Belief in British Public Life (CORAB) in 2015, convened by the Woolf Institute, stated that:

> The absence of a registered civil marriage in addition to the Nikah ceremony has led to a number of Muslim women, after a Muslim divorce, being deprived of any recourse to the matrimonial financial legislation available in the UK, and being therefore treated as having been in a state of cohabitation with their partner.[10]

The report called for further academic research on the experience and impact of tribunal decisions on women. It also said that the Ministry of Justice should disseminate best practice and examine whether 'marriage between members of minority religious groups should be required first or simultaneously to be registered according to English law' and whether religious tribunals should be 'required to have structures and processes compatible with arbitration legislation' (paras 8.27 and 8.28).

---

[10] Woolf Institute, *Living with Difference: Community, Diversity and the Common Good* (Report of the Commission on Religion and Belief in British Public Life, 2015) para 8.17.

Independent Review into the Application of Sharia Law in England and Wales

A 'key finding' of the Independent Review into the Application of Sharia Law in England and Wales in 2018 was that 'a significant number of Muslim couples fail to register their religious marriages', meaning that they have 'no option of obtaining a civil divorce'.[11] The Independent Review called for education, regulation of religious tribunals and legislation 'to ensure that civil marriages are conducted, before or at the same time as the Islamic marriage ceremony, bringing Islamic marriage in line with Christian and Jewish marriage in the eyes of the law'.[12]

Both the CORAB report and the Independent Review expressed a rather confused grasp of the law. The problem is not that there is a gap in protection. The Marriage Act 1949 already provides for Islamic marriage ceremonies to be legally binding, provided certain requirements are met. The problem is that those requirements for such marriage to occur in a place of worship indirectly discriminate against some religious traditions, such as Islam, where the tradition is otherwise. Arguing for the same treatment as for Christian and Jews is to argue for the status quo and will perpetuate rather than solve the problem. The Marriage Act 1949 already provides a means by which the religious marriage ceremony can occur at the same time as the legal ceremony.

Based on this misunderstanding of the law, the Independent Review proposed that 'legislative changes would be through amendments to the Marriage Act 1949 offences sections, so that the celebrant of any marriage, including Islamic marriages, would face penalties should they fail to ensure the

---

[11] Home Office, *The Independent Review into the Application of Sharia Law in England and Wales* (Cm 9560, 2018) 5.

[12] Ibid 17.

marriage is also civilly registered'.[13] It suggested that: 'This would make it a legal requirement for Muslim couples to civilly register their marriage before or at the same time as their Islamic ceremony'. Yet English law already requires civil registration in order for marriages to be legally binding. Under the current law, marriages that are not conducted under the Marriage Act 1949 do not have any legal effect. Under the Independent Review's proposals, they would be illegal. This would also criminalise marriage ceremonies by those who want a religious-only marriage as well as ceremonies conducted by non-religious bodies such as humanists and independent celebrants.

The Parliamentary Assembly of the Council of Europe

In January 2019 the Parliamentary Assembly of the Council of Europe passed a resolution expressing concern about the 'judicial' activities of 'Sharia Councils' in the United Kingdom.[14] The resolution noted that:

Although they are not considered part of the British legal system, Sharia councils attempt to provide a form of alternative dispute resolution, whereby members of the Muslim community, sometimes voluntarily, often under considerable social pressure, accept their religious jurisdiction mainly in marital and Islamic divorce issues, but also in matters relating to inheritance and Islamic commercial contracts. The Assembly is concerned that the rulings of the Sharia councils clearly discriminate against women in divorce and inheritance cases.

---

[13] Ibid 5.

[14] See Russell Sandberg and Frank Cranmer, 'The Council of Europe and *Sharia*: An Unsatisfactory Resolution?' (2019) 21 (2) *Ecclesiastical Law Journal* 203.

This neatly identifies the problem. However, the resolution became less accurate when it discussed how this problem was to be redressed. In this respect the resolution was influenced by and sought to implement the findings of the Independent Review. The resolution called on the authorities of the United Kingdom to take various actions, including to 'review the Marriage Act to make it a legal requirement for Muslim couples to civilly register their marriage before or at the same time as their Islamic ceremony, as is already stipulated by law for Christian and Jewish marriages' and to 'take appropriate enforcement measures to oblige the celebrant of any marriage, including Islamic marriages, to ensure that the marriage is also civilly registered before or at the same time as celebrating the religious marriage'. This again misunderstands the Marriage Act 1949: the Act already makes it a legal requirement for Muslims to register their marriages, the problem is the hurdles placed in the way of Muslims by the Act.

Yet the government welcomed the Independent Review, apart from its proposal to provide a regulation scheme for Sharia councils.[15] Oddly, this was rejected on the basis that it 'would confer upon them legitimacy as alternative forms of dispute resolution'. However, this is exactly how Sharia councils operate: they adjudicate disputes brought to them by individuals. As Gillian Douglas has noted, given the 'the general de-juridification of family matters and the drive to encourage alternative dispute resolution' as furthered by the cuts to legal aid as a result of the Legal Aid, Sentencing and Punishment of Offenders Act 2012:

> It is hard to see why religious tribunals should not be as suitable as any other potential mediator or arbitrator to assist the parties in reaching a settlement that suits them,

---

[15] HM Government, *Integrated Communities Strategy Green Paper* (March 2018) 58.

even if that settlement is one that reflects cultural or religious norms at odds with those of secular society.[16]

The problem with unregistered religious marriages is that the lack of legal recognition and redress from the State means that there is no an alternative option to the use of Sharia councils. Sharia councils become problematic where, rather, than being an alternative form of dispute resolution, they become the only option.

In contrast, the government endorsed the other recommendations made by the Independent Review and has begun work to 'explore the legal and practical challenges of limited reform in relation to the law on marriage and religious weddings'.[17] This work is ongoing and separate from the work of the Law Commission. However, the government's response to a consultation noted that 'many respondents focused on religious marriage reform and suggested that this will infringe on the rights of faith groups and shows a focus on Muslim groups'.[18] It is notable that this response did not refer to any legislative plans. However, a series of private Member's bills have been proposed by Baroness Cox which seek to enact the Independent Review's proposal for a new offence criminalising celebrants of religious marriages.

Criminalising celebrants

The Marriage Act 1949 (Amendment) Bill was not the first private Member's bill to be introduced by Baroness Cox to

---

[16] Gillian Douglas, 'Who Regulates Marriage? The Case of Religious Marriage and Divorce', in Russell Sandberg (ed), *Religion and Legal Pluralism* (Ashgate, 2015) 53, 61–2.

[17] HM Government, *Integrated Communities Strategy Green Paper* (March 2018) 58.

[18] HM Government, *Integrated Communities Strategy Green Paper: Summary of Consultation and Responses and Government Responses* (February 2019) 21.

deal with the issues raised by Sharia councils. Her previous Bill, the Arbitration and Mediation Services (Equality) Bill, was first introduced into the House of Lords in June 2011 and was repeatedly reintroduced with slight amendments until 2017, never becoming law.[19] That Bill sought to regulate the operation of religious tribunals by creating a new criminal offence of falsely purporting to 'exercise of any of the powers or duties of a court, or in the case of a purported arbitration, to make legally binding rulings without any basis whatsoever under the Arbitration Act 1996'. This proposed offence would have been ineffective, given that religious tribunals (or at least those that are known about in the empirical literature) do not operate under the Arbitration Act and do not falsely purport (or indeed purport at all) to have an authority equivalent to that exercised by the courts of the State.

This misunderstanding of the legal position and the rush to criminal sanction to provide a magic-bullet solution to the problem also underlies Baroness Cox's later Bill, the Marriage Act 1949 (Amendment) Bill, introduced in the parliamentary session of 2017–19, and with a slightly different version introduced for the 2019–21 session. This private Member's bill – which has little chance of becoming law without government support – seeks to amend the Marriage Act to make it an offence to purport to solemnise an unregistered religious marriage. It would make just the one amendment, inserting a new section 75(2B) which would provide:

Any person who knowingly and wilfully purports to solemnize a marriage (not being a marriage according to the rites of the Church of England, a marriage according to

---

[19] Sharon Thompson and Russell Sandberg, 'Common Defects of the Divorce Bill and the Arbitration and Mediation Services (Equality) Bill' (2017) *Family Law* 447.

the usages of the Society of Friends or marriage between two persons professing the Jewish religion according to the usages of the Jews) of two persons whose marriage has not been registered, and is not registered during the course of the solemnization, commits an offence punishable on summary conviction by a fine.

The 2017–19 version of the Bill, by contrast, sought to make a number of amendments to the Marriage Act 1949, which culminated in a provision that stated: 'Any person who knowingly and wilfully purports to solemnize a marriage which may not be lawfully registered pursuant to Parts I to IV of this Act shall be guilty of a felony and shall be liable to imprisonment for a term not exceeding five years.' While the reduction of the sentence is welcome, there remains the question of whether such an offence is necessary and whether this offence would deal with the issue of unregistered marriages. The proposed offence would penalise celebrants – 'any person who knowingly and wilfully purports to solemnize a marriage'. This focus on the criminalisation of celebrants is wrong in principle and the drafting of the Bill as it currently stands would not resolve concerns about unregistered marriages, for a number of reasons. First, it ignores the reasons why religious marriages may not be registered. The main issue is not that celebrants are deliberately failing to or colluding not to register marriages. Rather it is that some couples are having either deliberately or accidentally to have a religious marriage that does not comply with the law on marriage registration. Using the criminal law against a celebrant (assuming a celebrant can be identified) does not deal with the issue.

The crucial distinction is that made in the January 2019 Parliamentary Assembly of the Council of Europe Resolution between situations where couples submit voluntarily and, alternatively, where they submit under social pressure. Where the decision to use a religious authority for dispute resolution is genuinely voluntary on the part of both parties, then this should be no more objectionable than any other form of alternative dispute resolution. And similarly, the courts should not enforce any adjudication where submission to the authority was not voluntary – as is the case in relation to arbitration under the Arbitration Act 1996.

The issue with unregistered religious marriages arises only where the decision not to comply with the Marriage Act 1949 is unwitting or involuntary on the part of one or both of the parties. The offence proposed in the Cox Bill will not help in such a scenario. The problem with the offence is that it is focused on celebrants. Criminalising and fining celebrants would not extend the rights or protection afforded to those within unregistered marriages. It does little, if anything, to increase the level of awareness. Creating a criminal offence would be very heavy-handed and is a solution to a completely different problem to that identified in the Independent Review and the wider literature. If there were evidence that celebrants were deliberately not registering marriages, then this might be the solution. Criminalising religious marriages would make sense only if there was a fear of rogue celebrants forcing people to undergo religious ceremonies and falsely stating that such ceremonies resulted in legal marriages. However, there is no evidence of this (and if there were, then this could presumably be caught by the general provisions of the Fraud Act 2006). The only effect of this provision might be indirect: celebrants, over time, may become reluctant to engage in unregistered religious marriages. Moreover, this is an insufficient response to the problem. It would also make no distinction between those who voluntarily or involuntarily (wittingly or unwittingly) sought a non-registered marriage and the reasons why such a status might be sought. It is also likely to be the case that those who coerce their partners into unregistered religious marriages are likely to simply refuse to enter into registered marriages, leaving their partners in the same legal position. The offence would also be divisive in that, despite being generally worded, it would be seen as a very extreme measure directed at the Muslim community.[20]

Moreover, the criminal offence as currently drafted would be ineffective. This would be because of the requirement that the defendant 'knowingly and wilfully purports to solemnize a marriage'. This would limit the offence to where celebrants are deliberately claiming to conduct legal marriages where those marriages are not already registered or would not be registered as a result of the solemnisation. There is no suggestion that this is the issue that needs to be solved. The issue is, rather, that ceremonies are taking place that are outside the scope of the Act entirely: not that ceremonies are claiming or giving the impression that they are within the scope of the Act. The wording of the offence would also mean that it would be easily circumvented, provided that the celebrant did not 'purport to solemnise a marriage'. For instance, if the celebrant claimed that they were solemnising a religious wedding or a blessing, not a legal marriage, then their actions would fall outside the offence. The celebrant in such a situation could be said to be knowingly and wilfully ignoring the law and failing to share this with the parties. The celebrant could also be knowingly and wilfully helping one of the parties to avoid a legally registered marriage. Yet, the celebrant would not be liable. To remedy this, the offence needs to be recast to include the situation where celebrants have not checked or are negligent about whether the marriages are not already registered or would not be registered as a result of the solemnisation. The word 'purports' needs to be removed so that it does not need to be proved that the defendant implied that the ceremony was within the scope of the Marriage Act.

---

[20] Rajnaara C. Akhtar, 'Religious-only Marriage and Cohabitation: Deciphering Differences', in Rajnaara C. Akhtar, Patrick Nash and Rebecca Probert (eds), *Cohabitation and Religious Marriage* (Bristol University Press, 2020) 69, 76–8.

In any case, the Marriage Act 1949 (Amendment) Bill does not deal with the correct mischief. The focus on criminalising and fining celebrants misses the point: the issue is with the parties, not with the celebrant. Not only would the criminal offence envisaged by the Act be ineffective, but it also highlights that criminal sanction on its own will not provide a solution to the unregistered marriage issue. Indeed, there is unlikely to be one magic-bullet solution to the issue. This has been underlined by recent litigation where a Family Court judge attempted to deal with the problem by an imaginative reinterpretation of the law on validity, but, as we will see, this has been slapped down on Appeal.

Akhter v Khan

The facts of *Akhter v Khan* relate to a typical unregistered religious marriage. In 1998, Nasreen Akhter and Mohammed Shabaz Khan had a nikah ceremony. They intended to register the marriage under civil law, but never got around to it, and indeed as time went on Khan refused to register it. They had four children together, and while they lived in Dubai between 2005 and 2011 they were considered by the authorities there to be validly married. After 18 years, and back in the UK, the relationship broke down in 2016 and Akhter issued a petition for divorce from Khan.

At first instance, Mr Justice Williams noted that the case law had established a three-fold distinction: 'as the law currently stands a marriage can not only be valid and void but also what has become termed a non-marriage'.[21] He held that there was no question whether the Islamic marriage ceremony should be treated as creating a valid marriage in English law. However, somewhat creatively he held that it had been a void marriage rather than a 'non-marriage'. A marriage can

---

[21] *Akhter v Khan* [2018] EWFC 54, para 6.

be annulled as void where parties had failed to comply with certain requirements as to the formation of marriage.[22] The importance of this distinction is as follows: Parties to a void marriage enjoy the same benefits as a married couple until the marriage is annulled, and once a marriage is annulled then they are able to go to the State courts for assistance dividing their assets. By contrast, if there had been a 'non-marriage', then this would have meant that they would have had no recourse to State law on relationship breakdown.

Williams J noted that where a couple had undergone a public marriage ceremony and had 'lived a married life and been accepted as married by their communities', then designating this as a non-marriage felt 'instinctively uncomfortable … and might rightly be regarded as insulting by many' (para 8). He held that 'the expression non-marriage should be reserved only to those situations such as acting or children playing where there has never been any intention to genuinely create a marriage' (para 81). For Williams J, there was a need to take a holistic view of a process rather than focusing on a single ceremony (para 94). He held that the marriage was void because there was an intention to follow up the religious wedding with a ceremony that complied with marriage law. Human rights supported a finding of a decree of a void marriage 'in respect of those who sought to effect or intended to effect a legal marriage' and it was a relevant factor 'whether the failure to complete all the legal formalities was a joint decision or due to the failure of one party to complete them' (paras 80, 94).

The Attorney General appealed. (Neither the petitioner nor the respondent took any active part in this appeal because they had reached an agreed settlement). The Court of Appeal allowed the appeal reversing the decision of Williams J and re-establishing the previous position that Williams J's flexibility

---

[22] Matrimonial Causes Act 1973, s11(a)(iii).

sought to circumvent.[23] The Court of Appeal ruled that there was, in this case, 'no ceremony in respect of which a decree of nullity could be granted' (para 128). They insisted that there needed to be a ceremony under the Marriage Act which suffered from a defect in order for there to be a void marriage. They agreed with what they termed 'Williams J's disquiet about the use of the term "non-marriage" (para 7)'. However, they suggested that 'a better way of describing the legal consequences of what has happened is to use the expression, "non-qualifying ceremony"' to signify that the relationships 'are outside the scope of both the 1949 and the 1973 Acts' and to stress 'that the focus should be on the ceremony' (para 64).

While Williams J had focused on the unfairness of the category of non-marriage, the Court of Appeal was more concerned with preserving the certainty of the category of marriage. They insisted that the question of 'whether a ceremony created a valid marriage or a void marriage or was of no legal effect at all must be determined at the date of the ceremony' (para 124). It could not 'depend on whether the parties might have agreed to undertake a further step or steps', since this 'might result in a party being married even when they had changed their mind part way through the process' (para 126). No one can be forced to marry, and, indeed, forcing someone to marry is a criminal offence (para 88).

The Court of Appeal was correct to highlight these problems with the flexible and holistic approach developed by Williams J. However, in removing Williams J's solution to the unregistered religious marriage issue it is clear that the problem of unregistered religious marriages still remains. The Court of Appeal confirmed that unregistered religious marriages are to be regarded as 'non-qualifying ceremonies' that are outside the scope of marriage and divorce legislation. The case highlights

---

[23] *Her Majesty's Attorney General v Akhter* [2020] EWCA Civ 122.

the need to provide redress for those who are in unregistered religious marriages either where this is unwitting on the part of one or both of the parties or where this is not agreed by one of the parties (such as in this case where the husband promised that they would comply with marriage registration laws at a later date). Moreover, the difficulties with the purposive reasoning of Williams J suggest that reform to mitigate (if not solve) this problem needs to come from Parliament rather than from judicial activism.

Conclusion

This chapter has documented the fast rise in concern about unregistered religious marriages. Empirical studies and official reports agree that unregistered religious marriages are problematic in that parties are denied remedies under State law on relationship breakdown.[24] This poses particular issues where this means that forms of religious-based adjudication become the only option for resolving separation disputes rather than a form of alternative dispute resolution. There is no consensus, however, as to the best way to deal with or at least mitigate this. One popular suggestion, as championed by the Independent Review, recommended by the Council of Europe resolution and elucidated in Baroness Cox's Bill, has been to create a criminal offence on those who solemnise religious weddings that fail to comply with the Marriage Act 1949. However, this would do nothing for those who are already in unregistered religious marriages and is likely to be an ineffective way of preventing the number of such marriages in the future. Likewise, the *Akhter v Khan* decisions show that purposive

---

[24] They seldom mention that cuts to legal aid have limited access to such remedies. On which see, for example, Jess Mant and Julie Wallbank, 'The Mysterious Case of Disappearing Family Law and the Shrinking Vulnerable Subject' (2017) 26 (5) *Social and Legal Studies* 629.

reasoning and judicial activism using the law of validity are unlikely to provide a fix.

The heart of the problem of unregistered religious marriages can be found in the complex and indirectly discriminatory legal framework which has failed to keep up with societal changes. This suggests that the path ahead is not only updating the provisions of the Marriage Act 1949 but looking at the entire legal framework affecting intimate adult relationships. Criminal offences and changes to the law on validity may play a part, but only within a wider, more comprehensive reform. Moreover, such reform would respond not only to the unregistered religious marriages issue but also to other pressing needs such as the general need for cohabitation rights and, as will be discussed in the next chapter, the current exclusion of non-religious marriages from the Marriage Act 1949.

FIVE

Non-Religious Marriages

Introduction

This chapter explores the other main concern that has arisen in recent years: the exclusion of non-religious belief marriages under the Marriage Act 1949. This chapter will fall into three sections. The first will introduce the issue, while the second will examine how this issue has arisen in the public debate, exploring the campaign of Humanists UK during the parliamentary passage of the Marriage (Same Sex Couples) Act 2013 and subsequent legal and political developments. The final section will then discuss the High Court challenge of the current law in *R (On Application of Harrison) v Secretary of State for Justice*,[1] which concluded that the law interfered with the applicant's human rights but that this was justified by the fact that the law was currently under review by the Law Commission.

The context

English law has struggled with the recognition of non-religious beliefs. This is reflected in a series of unprincipled and contra-dictory Employment Tribunal decisions on how belief is to be

---

[1]   [2020] EWHC 2096 (Admin).

defined for the purpose of employment law. Beliefs in independence for Scotland[2] and veganism[3] have been protected, while the wearing of a poppy[4] and vegetarianism[5] have not, for instance.[6] In relation to marriage law, the problem is rather different: non-religious belief systems are simply excluded. Section 41(1) of the Marriage Act 1949 provides that a 'proprietor or trustee of a building, which has been certified as required by law as a place of religious worship may apply ... for the building to be registered for the solemnization of marriages therein'. The provision of protection only on grounds of religion is socially, politically and legally outmoded.

A report by an All Party Parliamentary Humanist Group in 2018 suggested that until the 1970s a blind eye had been turned to the issue and weddings conducted by belief groups were considered to be legally binding.[7] According to the report, 'some ethical societies performed wedding ceremonies in their venues, and relatively lax interpretations of the law at the time meant that these generally had legal recognition'. The report noted that 'this continued until the anomalous position was picked up by Government officials in the 1970s'. The Court of Appeal decision in *R v Registrar General, ex parte Segerdal*[8] then provided the common law definition of place of religious worship (to refuse an application by the Church of Scientology). And in *Re South Place Ethical Society, Barralet v AG*,[9] this was applied in the context of charitable status to hold

---

[2]   *McEleny v MOD* [2018] UKET 4105347/2017.

[3]   *Casamitjana v The League of Cruel Sports* [2020] ET 3331129/2018.

[4]   *Lisk v Shield Guardian Co Ltd & Others* [2011] ET 3300873/2011.

[5]   *Mr G Conisbee v Crossley Farms Ltd & Ors* [2019] ET 3335357/2018.

[6]   See Russell Sandberg 'Is the National Health Service a Religion?' (2020) 22 *Ecclesiastical Law Journal* 343.

[7]   All-Party Parliamentary Humanist Group, *'Any Lawful Impediment?' A Report of the All-Party Parliamentary Humanist Group's Inquiry into the Legal Recognition of Humanist Marriage in England and Wales* (2018) 11.

[8]   [1970] 2 QB 679.

[9]   [1980] 1 WLR 1565.

that a belief organisation, the South Place Ethical Society was not charitable for the advancement of religion because there was no 'worship in the sense which worship is an attribute of religion': it was 'not possible to worship in that way a mere ethical or philosophical ideal'.[10]

These two cases provided the common law definition of religion until the case of *R (on the Application of Hodkin) v Registrar General of Births, Deaths and Marriages*,[11] which put forward a new definition of 'a place of meeting for religious worship' (and held that the Church of Scientology was now included by that definition) but held that this definition only include 'spiritual or non-secular belief' systems. Lord Toulson held that the exclusion of secular belief systems was appropriate because there are other legal provisions which allow for secular wedding services on approved premises.[12] However, this contention rested on the assumption that a civil wedding is an appropriate substitute for humanists. The All-Party Parliamentary Humanist Group report rejected this, adopting Humanists UK's definition of a humanist wedding as:

A non-religious ceremony that is deeply personal and conducted by a humanist celebrant. It differs from a civil wedding in that it is entirely hand-crafted and reflective of the humanist beliefs and values of the couple, conducted by a celebrant who shares their beliefs and values, and can take place in any venue that is special to them.[13]

This definition highlights that couples who seek a wedding ceremony conducted by a humanist, or other belief-organisation

---

[10] At 1573.

[11] [2013] UKSC 77.

[12] Paras 58–59.

[13] All-Party Parliamentary Humanist Group, *'Any Lawful Impediment?' A Report of the All-Party Parliamentary Humanist Group's Inquiry into the Legal Recognition of Humanist Marriage in England and Wales* (2018) 6.

ceremony, are unlikely to be satisfied by a civil ceremony. Yet, under the Marriage Act 1949, couples who have a humanist wedding ceremony must have a separate civil marriage in order for their marriage to be legally binding. As the All-Party Parliamentary Humanist Group report pointed out, this is 'costly and an administrative burden' and not only can this put 'such couples at a serious disadvantage, financially and practically, in terms of their ability to have the wedding they want' but it 'also means that many couples feel aggrieved that what they see as their "real" wedding is not recognised as such in the eyes of the law'.[14] There is a clear demand for non-religious wedding ceremonies. The report noted that Humanists UK celebrants performed over 1,000 ceremonies in England and Wales in 2016. Moreover, the Scottish experience shows that if such ceremonies were legally binding, then they would be significantly more popular. In Scotland, belief marriages were given legal status in 2005 and by 2018 the number of humanist ceremonies had overtaken the number of Church of Scotland ceremonies, becoming the largest type of marriage outside civil registrations.[15] The campaign for legal recognition has stepped up in recent years, largely as a result of campaigns during the parliamentary passage of the Marriage (Same Sex Couples) Act 2013 which were to provide a limited success.

Legislative manoeuvres

Reform of the law of marriage was mooted several times during the 20th century,[16] as well as under the Blair government when a move from registering buildings to appointing

---

[14] Ibid 19, 5.

[15] National Records of Scotland, *Vital Events Reference Tables 2019*. Section 7: Marriages and Civil Partnerships, Table 7.07: 'Marriages, by denomination, Scotland, 2019'.

[16] See Stephen Cretney, *Family Law in the Twentieth Century: A History* (Oxford University Press, 2003).

celebrants was considered, but stalled because it was thought too important to enact by secondary legislation and there was no suitable Bill before Parliament to include such suggestions.[17] During this period, Humanists UK made a strong argument for ceremonies conducted by humanist celebrants to be included as part of any reform and it was considered that the government had now 'recognised the case for reform, and proposed further investigation and consultation'.[18] However, with the election of the Coalition government, no further work materialised and the humanists looked at other ways to achieve their goals.

In 2012 a private Member's bill was introduced. Lord Harrison's Marriage (Approved Organisations) Bill 2012–13 was noteworthy in terms of how it sought to deal with the issue: there was no move away from registering buildings; rather, what was proposed was a piecemeal reform which, according to the All-Party Parliamentary Humanist Group report, 'operated by replicating as closely as possible the provisions found in the Marriage Act 1949 for the Society of Friends'. It permitted recognition to all religious and non-religious groups without a registered place of worship provided that they were registered as a charity for the advancement of religion or belief and that the group 'appears to the Registrar General to be of good repute'. Although Lord Harrison's Bill did not have a second reading, the All-Party Parliamentary Humanist Group claims that it 'laid the groundwork for subsequent debates during the passage of the Marriage (Same Sex Couples) Act 2013'.[19]

---

[17] Written comment, House of Commons Hansard, 1 March 2005, vol 431, col 77WS.

[18] All-Party Parliamentary Humanist Group, *'Any Lawful Impediment?' A Report of the All-Party Parliamentary Humanist Group's Inquiry into the Legal Recognition of Humanist Marriage in England and Wales* (2018) 12.

[19] Ibid 13.

Identical amendments were introduced at the committee stage of the Marriage (Same Sex Couples) Bill in February 2013 but were rejected by the government on the basis that the subjective 'good repute' test would make the Registrar General 'particularly vulnerable' and that the Bill was not the right vehicle for reform, given that others may also wish to marry outdoors. Then, at report stage in the Commons the amendments were redrafted to only cover humanism only. The amendments referred only to registered charities 'principally concerned with advancing or practising the non-religious belief known as humanism', and required that the charities had been in continuous existence for five years and appeared to be of good repute. Although the report says that this change in focus was suggested by the government,[20] ironically, in debate this new focus came under attack by the then Attorney General, Dominic Grieve, who expressed concern that the clause 'would render the Bill incompatible with the provisions of the European Convention on Human Rights, because it identifies a group that is not a religious group and gives it a special status'.[21]

The amendment was withdrawn, but at committee stage in the House of Lords a new amendment was tabled, this time focusing on non-religious belief systems. It was addressed to charities 'principally concerned with advancing or practising a non-religious belief' which had been in existence for ten years but had 'been performing celebrations of marriage and other ceremonies for its members for at least five years, such ceremonies being rooted in its belief system', had 'in place written procedures for the selection, training and accreditation of persons to conduct solemnisations of marriages' and met the good repute test.[22] The government spokesperson, Baroness

---

[20] Ibid 13–14.

[21] House of Commons Hansard, 21 May 2013, col 563.

[22] All-Party Parliamentary Humanist Group, *'Any Lawful Impediment?' A Report of the All-Party Parliamentary Humanist Group's Inquiry into the Legal Recognition of Humanist Marriage in England and Wales* (2018) 15–16.

Stowell, responded by professing that 'of course everyone would support humanist marriages' but that 'it would require a change in law that would have implications that have not yet been fully thought through'.[23]

The saga reached its end at report stage in the Lords. A new amendment mandated the Secretary of State to make regulations within six months to 'make provision for the Registrar General to approve and permit organisations that are registered charities principally concerned with advancing or practising a non-religious belief to solemnise marriages according to their usages on the authority of a superintendent registrar's certificate'.[24] Baroness Stowell also tabled an amendment to mandate a review of whether an order should be made to permit 'marriages according to the usages of belief organisations to be solemnized on the authority of certificates of a superintendent registrar' and to allow the Secretary of State to make provision by order to permit such marriages.

This second amendment proved successful and became section 14 of the Marriage (Same Sex Couples) Act 2013. This required a review to be produced and published by 1 January 2015, allowed for an order to amend legislation in England and Wales, stipulated that any order 'must provide that no religious service may be used at a marriage which is solemnised in pursuance of the order' and defined 'belief organisation' as 'an organisation whose principal or sole purpose is the advancement of a system of non-religious beliefs which relate to morality or ethics'. This provision not only suggested that the argument in favour of such an amendment had been won but also showed how the debate had moved on during the passage of the Marriage (Same Sex Couples) Act 2013. Rather

---

[23] House of Lords Hansard, 19 June 2013, col 311.

[24] All-Party Parliamentary Humanist Group, *'Any Lawful Impediment?' A Report of the All-Party Parliamentary Humanist Group's Inquiry into the Legal Recognition of Humanist Marriage in England and Wales* (2018) 16.

than providing recognition to all religious and non-religious groups without a registered place or worship (provided that they were registered as a charity and held in good repute) – a move which would also go some way towards mitigating the problem of unregistered religious marriages – now recognition was sought solely for 'belief organisations' as a further category under the Marriage Act 1949 closely replicating the position of Quakers.

The review required by section 14 was duly carried out by the Ministry of Justice, reporting in December 2014.[25] The majority of respondents were in favour of changing the law (para 14). However, although fewer respondents answered the follow-up questions in the consultation, the majority of those who did thought that 'qualifying tests' such as charitable status, being well established and requiring at least one of the marrying couple to be a member of the registered organisation should be applied but that 'it would be difficult or impossible to apply certain types of criteria without the risk of discriminating against some belief organisations' (para 13). This gave reason for the Ministry of Justice to pause, pointing out that responses raised 'a number of complex issues' with 'implications for marriage solemnization more broadly' and that there was a need to ask the Law Commission to begin 'a broader review of the law concerning marriage ceremonies' which would 'be able to examine all the issues arising from the consultation alongside all other relevant matters' (paras 15, 20).

The fact that this was the 'immediate catalyst' for the Law Commission's work in this area explains the scope of that work: the Law Commission was asked not to look at the law on intimate adult relationships as a whole; it was not even asked to look at the law on marriage generally; rather, its

---

[25] Ministry of Justice, *Marriages by Non-Religious Belief Organisations: Summary of Written Responses to the Consultation and Government Response* (2014).

scope was the law on 'getting married'.[26] In its 2015 scoping paper, the Law Commission sought to 'identify the questions that any future reform project would address' (para 1.40). The Law Commission concluded that there was a 'clear need for reform' but agreed with the Ministry of Justice consultation response that there was 'no simple solution that would solve the range of problems in the law that we have identified' (para 1.50). It concluded that any steps to reform the law to accommodate marriages by non-religious organisations needed 'to take place alongside a broader updating of the law of marriage that seeks to address a number of long-standing problems'. This call for 'a full Law Commission reform project' went unanswered for a number of years until a two-year project was announced in June 2019. The resulting consultation paper, published in September 2020, will be examined in the next chapter.

Ironically, the two reviews shifted the debate in the reverse direction compared to the various amendments made during the passage of the Marriage (Same Sex Couples) Act 2013: now the direction was away from specific piecemeal reform to deal with non-religious belief marriages and towards wider reform of marriage law. However, humanists were reluctant to wait for such wider reform. As the All-Party Parliamentary Humanist Group report noted 'while piecemeal legislation is generally undesirable, it appears that wholesale reform is not on the table – and even if it was, it would take years'.[27] They stressed that Humanists UK was 'not pushing for a celebrant-based system. What Humanists UK has told us it wants – and what the existing Order-making power allows – is a position akin to that already held by the Quakers, i.e. organisation-based

---

[26] Law Commission, *Getting Married: A Scoping Paper* (2015) para 1.37.

[27] All-Party Parliamentary Humanist Group, *'Any Lawful Impediment?' A Report of the All-Party Parliamentary Humanist Group's Inquiry into the Legal Recognition of Humanist Marriage in England and Wales* (2018) 6.

recognition.'[28] The humanists therefore returned to the approach that they had used prior to the passage of the Marriage (Same Sex Couples) Act 2013, a private Member's bill. Baroness Meacher's Marriage (Approved Organisations) Bill included the power for the Secretary of State to 'authorise further belief organisations'. This was introduced in the House of Lords for a first reading on 9 February 2020, while the Marriage (Approved Belief Organisations) Bill, sponsored by Rehman Chishti, received its first reading on 22 October 2020. In between these two dates, however, the context had shifted considerably. Not only had the Law Commission published it consultation paper proposing for a wider reform of weddings law but also the matter of humanist weddings had gone to court.

R (On Application of Harrison) v Secretary of State for Justice

Just months before the Law Commission's consultation paper was due to be published, a challenge was brought before the High Court by six couples – supported by Humanists UK – against the current prohibition on humanist weddings. In a briefing to MPs, Humanists UK pointed out that while the Law Commission could 'make recommendations on how humanist marriages could be recognised, it can't recommend to the Government if they should be'.[29] In the end, the decision in *R (On Application of Harrison) v Secretary of State for Justice*[30] indicated that the law should change but did not go quite as far as to require immediate change. Ironically, given the stance of the humanist campaign, the High Court held

---

[28] Ibid 41.

[29] Humanists UK, https://humanism.org.uk/briefing-for-mps-on-humanist-marriages-in-england-and-wales/

[30] [2020] EWHC 2096 (Admin).

that the only reason that stopped a declaration that the current law was discriminatory and incompatible with human rights was the current and ongoing work of the Law Commission, because the decision to look at the issue within the contest of wider reform was justified.

The claimants had alleged that the Marriage Act 1949 breached their rights under Article 14 of the European Convention on Human Rights (which provides a right not to be discriminated against in the exercise of Convention rights) taken together with Article 8 (respect for private and family life), Article 9 (freedom of religion or belief) and Article 12 (right to marry) and sought a Declaration of Incompatibility under the Human Rights Act 1998.[31] The Secretary of State maintained that there had been no breach of Convention rights, since the law on civil marriage provided a legally recognised, non-religious ceremony that was sufficiently capable of accommodating the claimants' wishes and beliefs. He further considered that even if there had been any difference in treatment between the claimants and their religious comparators, the measures under challenge were 'objectively and reasonably justified, not least given ongoing consideration of reform in this area of social policy' (para 4).

Eady J disagreed and held that the facts of the case fell within the ambit of Article 9. A measure need not go to the 'core of the right' to fall within its ambit; rather, it is sufficient 'if it has a more than tenuous connection with the core values it seeks to protect' (paras 65, 69). Indeed, the evidence that for many who hold humanist beliefs, 'ceremonies that mark significant life events, such as marriage, provide a close and direct link to the beliefs of the participants' would be enough

---

[31] In the event of the courts issuing a declaration of incompatibility, the current law prevails subject to a 'fast-track' system of executive action to bring English law into line with the Convention: Human Rights Act 1998 ss4 and 10.

for a wish to hold such ceremonies to constitute a manifest-ation of Article 9, which would go further than being within its ambit. By contrast, the Article 8 argument was dismissed on the basis that their compliant did not demonstrate 'more than a tenuous connection with the core values' of Article 8, given that the claimants were able to enter into marriages that had legal recognition (para 70). Eady J further held that this there had been a discriminatory difference of treatment between the claimants and religious comparators. The differential treatment in this case was that 'unlike their religious comparators, a marriage ceremony according to their humanist beliefs will not be legally recognised absent the supervisory presence of state officials' (para 93) . There is no option for humanist celebrants to take on the role played by the Superintendent Registrar and Registrar in civil weddings. Eady J noted that this issue had been termed in the litigation the 'unwanted guests problem' and that this was a 'difference of substance' (paras 89 and 94).

Eady J held that such discrimination could not be justified on grounds of 'the special place of marriage and of particular marriage ceremonies to the religions in question', since that would 'simply repeat the discrimination of which the claimants complain' and because there was 'no rational connection between the way in which English law recognises marriage and the stated objective' (paras 93, 105). Neither could the current position be justified on grounds that creating a new separate category of marriage ceremony for humanists would add further complexity and would introduce new forms of discrimination against non-humanists or non-belief systems: it was 'no defence to plead that the system is already discrim-inatory and no answer to rely on a possible risk of some new, hypothetical discrimination as justification for the very real adverse impact already suffered' (paras 106, 110).

However, the current discrimination was justified by the 'legitimate aim not to wish to reform the law in a piecemeal fashion when there are further issues arising in this area of social policy (presently being considered by the Law Commission) and that the Government and then Parliament should be allowed time to reflect' (para 107). It was relevant that the Law Commission concurred with the government's view, that reform was needed on a wholesale, rather than piecemeal, basis. Eady J noted that:

> Although I may deprecate the delay that has occurred since 2015, I cannot ignore the fact that there is currently an on-going review of the law of marriage in this country that will necessarily engage with the wider concerns that have been raised. Given these circumstances, at this time, the defendant has demonstrated that a fair balance has been struck between the individual rights of the Claimants and those of the broader community. (para 128)

The judgment therefore erected a distinction between giving recognition to humanist marriage and pursuing wholesale reform. However, this does not explain why a declaration of incompatibility was not awarded: such a declaration would not have mandated instant recognition of humanist marriage but would have provided a strong legal basis upon which such recognition would need to have been made as part of wholesale reform. Further litigation might be necessary in the future to achieve this if the Law Commission's proposals are not enacted in a way that facilitates non-religious marriages.

Conclusion

The absence of the legal recognition of non-religious marriages cannot be justified socially, politically, legally or practically, given the number of ceremonies that are already carried out and that such ceremonies are given legal effect in neighbouring jurisdictions. As Eady J noted in *Harrison*, Humanists UK is already 'the fifth largest provider of religious or belief-based wedding ceremonies, after the Church of England, the Roman

Catholic Church, the Church in Wales and the Methodist Church' (para 27). There has been little argument against the need for reform. The tale of the last decade has been how the humanist campaign has consistently *almost* got its way. Winning the argument was the easiest part: what has proved controversial is not so much whether such marriages should be legally recognised but how.

Comparing the 2012 and 2020 private Member's bills shows how far the humanist campaign has come in relation to that 'how' question. Despite the government and Law Commission shifting towards general reform of the law on how to get married – to some extent resurrecting the ideas that animated the aborted reform during the New Labour era – Humanists UK have moved in the opposite direction, seeking a specific remedy for belief organisations, stressing the human rights issues posed by protecting religions and not other beliefs and insisting on specific reform now.

One concern, expressed time and again, is the extent to which enabling belief organisations to lawfully solemnise marriages will replace one form of discrimination with another. In other words, where will the line be drawn? This comes back to the vexed question of how the term 'belief' is to be defined. However, it also asks the wider question of whether religion and belief organisations should be the only non-State bodies to conduct legally binding marriages. In recent years, a number of wedding ceremonies have been conducted by independent celebrants who offer non-legally binding ceremonies that are bespoke to the couple in question. Research by Stephanie Pywell suggests that such ceremonies reflect 'a growing trend for personalised wedding ceremonies which overcome strict religious/civil dichotomy' found in the Marriage Act 1949.[32]

---

[32] Stephanie Pywell, 'The Day of their Dreams: Celebrant-Led Wedding Celebration Ceremonies' [2020] *Child and Family Law Quarterly* 177;

Pywell noted that some couples wanted a ceremony which 'was principally secular, but included some words, readings, music or rituals based on religious or cultural tradition'. She argued that couples who sought such ceremonies were 'not opting out of marriage, but were expressing their dissatisfaction with the forms of marriage ceremony available to them. They were willing to organise – and pay for – two ceremonies in order to achieve the legal outcome that they wanted, and to participate in an event that they hoped would provide them with lifelong happy memories'. Her research found that the 'huge majority of couples' who had opted for such ceremonies did want to be legally married and they appreciated that their ceremony would not achieve this. Pywell found that 70–85% of couples were already married at the time of the ceremony, 10–19% stated that they intended to marry after the ceremony, 3–6% stated that they did not intend to marry, while the intentions of 1–4% were not known.

Many of the arguments for legally binding humanist marriages in terms of cost and choice apply also to independent celebrants. Although the human rights argument based on Article 9 is stronger in relation to humanist and other belief weddings, an argument could be made that denying interfaith marriages or otherwise blended religious and civil marriages does not allow for the manifestation of Article 9 rights. To make humanist and other belief organisations' wedding ceremonies legally binding while leaving those conducted by independent celebrants outside the law would simply be to move the line where discrimination occurs. Pywell suspected that the reason why independent celebrants had been ignored might be due to perception that they are commercial providers. She noted that it might be 'because their lack of a declared belief system is perceived as somehow diminishing the service

Stephanie Pywell, 'Beyond Beliefs: A Proposal to give Couples in England and Wales a Real Choice of Marriage Officiants' [2020] *Child and Family Law Quarterly* 215.

that they offer, or because – despite the fact that they cannot actually solemnise marriages – they are viewed by some as cynically cashing in on the vast sums of money that couples are prepared to spend on personalised, Instagram-friendly, ceremonies'. This is seemingly the position of Humanists UK, who declined the invitation to take part in her project on the grounds that their celebrants form 'a different category of ceremony providers': 'Our celebrants conduct ceremonies from a belief based, humanist, life-stance and are therefore not equivalent to the commercial celebrants this survey is addressing. Our comparators are those who conduct belief-based or religious weddings, legally recognised or not.' This issue of where to draw the line will apply regardless of whether reform is enacted on a piecemeal basis or whether wholesale reform is pursued. For Pywell, the main difference between humanist and independent celebrant ceremonies is that many independent celebrants 'offer couples a bespoke blend of secular and/or religious elements within one ceremony', while it was unlikely that humanist celebrants 'accredited by an avowedly non-religious organisation would feel able to do this'. Other than that, she noted that 'both categories appear to be well-organised and professional'. Indeed, many independent celebrants are not truly independent at all but are associated to umbrella organisations such as the Wedding Celebrancy Commission. These similarities notwithstanding, enabling independent celebrants to conduct lawfully binding marriages would represent a significant change in that it would mean that marriages could be solemnised by celebrants who are neither employed by the State nor representatives of religion or belief organisations. Indeed, if ceremonies by independent celebrants are legally binding, then it makes little sense to limit the organisations that can solemnise weddings to religion or belief organisations.

SIX

The Law Commission's Proposals

Introduction

The previous chapters have laid out the need for reform: the Marriage Act 1949 is unprincipled and unequal, providing a legal framework which is the product of historical quirk and not only reflects the Christian origins of marriage law but also indirectly discriminates against some religious traditions. The welcome progressive reforms of recent years have been bolted on to this antiquated framework in a way that makes the law overly complicated and also shows that the focus has been only on regulating particular forms of relationships. The antiquated, ineffective and unjust nature of the law has led to a number of marriages taking place extra-legally and this has led to two specific issues of concern: unregistered religious marriages and non-religious marriages. In short, the law on marriage no longer reflects the social reality of adult intimate relationships in the 21st century.

Given this, it is unsurprising that while the Law Commission's task for their scoping paper was to make the case for reform, their focus in their consultation paper has been instead to argue what reforms are needed.[1] This chapter explores and analyses

---

[1] Law Commission, *Getting Married: A Consultation Paper on Weddings Law* (Consultation Paper 247, 2020).

the reforms suggested by the Law Commission's consultation paper, published in September 2020, which proposes a transformation of the law on how people get married. The consultation paper proposes 'an officiant-focused scheme' which would replace the current law's focus on registered buildings. The Law Commission's main proposals can be summarised as follows.

- All weddings would be required to take place in the presence of one authorised officiant who would be responsible for ensuring that the legal requirements are met. The officiant could be, but would not need to be, the celebrant.
- The following could be officiants: (1) registration officers; (2) Anglican clergy; (3) nominated officiants from any religion or belief body; (4) independent officiants who apply directly to the General Register Office or Registrar General.
- Each of the couple would need to give at least 28 days' notice and this would take the form of two steps: (1) the initial giving of notice, which might take place remotely (for example, by post or online); and (2) an in-person meeting with a registration officer.
- Weddings would take place according to the form and ceremony chosen by the parties and agreed by the officiant. This could include weddings outside. The only requirement would be for the parties to express their consent to be married.
- There would be a valid marriage provided that (1) the couple have given notice, (2) both parties consent and (3) at least one of them believes that the person officiating at the ceremony is authorised to solemnise a legal marriage.
- It would be a criminal offence for any person to purport to be an officiant and to deliberately or recklessly mislead either of the couple about their status or the effect of the ceremony. It would also be an offence for an officiant deliberately or recklessly to mislead either of the couple about the effect of the ceremony.

This chapter falls into three parts. The first part introduces the Law Commission's approach and looks at what was excluded from its terms of reference and the main changes that are proposed to how people get married. The second part then discusses the most radical change proposed by the Law Commission: the move from the Marriage Act 1949's focus on registering buildings towards what the Law Commission has styled an officiant system and how this would accommodate non-religious marriages. The final part looks at how the scoping paper discussed the issue of unregistered religious marriages and the extent to which the reforms suggested would help to mitigate that issue, including an examination of what the Law Commission suggests in terms of the law on validity and on criminal offences concerning the solemnisation of marriage. Taken together, the proposals do not provide a magic-bullet solution but they do provide important steps forward. There are points of contention, but overall the proposals, if enacted, would provide a great deal of improvement.

Proposed changes to how people get married

The Law Commission's focus is on what they call 'weddings law', that is, 'the law which governs weddings: how and where couples can get married' (para 1.11). The Commission are not considering ' "marriage" itself, meaning the legal status of being married and the legal consequences that flow from it', including the law on eligibility to marriage, 'the duty of the Church of England and the Church in Wales to conduct marriage ceremonies of their parishioners' and the 'question of whether or not religious groups should be obliged to solemnize marriages of same-sex couples', which the agreed terms of reference stated 'was decided by Parliament following wide public debate' (para 17.4). Also excluded are some 'matters of policy that are reserved for Government or have been the subject of recent reforms' (para 1.14). These include the move towards a schedule system of registering marriages as well as the following two rather more controversial developments.

First, the Law Commission is 'not considering the recommendation of the Independent Review into the Application of Sharia Law in England and Wales to amend the Marriage Act 1949 so that celebrants of marriages would face penalties should they fail to ensure that the marriage is also civilly registered'. Yet, as will be discussed later, not only does the consultation paper explicitly raise and discuss the issue of unregistered religious marriages but it also makes recommendations in respect of criminal offences as well as exploring how their other proposals could mitigate the problem.

Second, the Law Commission is 'not considering whether non-religious belief organisations, including Humanists, and independent celebrants should be able to conduct legally binding weddings'. However, the Law Commission is 'considering, if they were permitted to conduct weddings, how they could be incorporated into a reformed law'. This means that the Commission's work does not 'consider the policy and legal arguments – including the human rights arguments – for and against expanding the class of groups that can conduct legally binding weddings' (para 5.8). However, this exclusion is slight, given that not only does the paper 'consider how a new system *could* include weddings conducted by non-religious belief organisations and independent celebrants if it were decided that the law should allow these groups to perform legally binding weddings' but also it ensures that their 'scheme is compatible with human rights law in its application to those groups who are permitted to conduct weddings – including any new groups to which it may apply' (para 5.9).

There is therefore an element of artificiality in relation to both of these exclusions. The consultation paper is very much concerned with the two issues of unregistered religious marriages and non-religious marriages discussed in the previous chapters.

The Law Commission concludes that the current law is an 'ancient and complex hodgepodge of different rules for different types of ceremonies', which leads to inefficiencies and unfairness: 'couples and communities face different rules and limitations, depending on the type of wedding ceremony, with some given more freedom to have a ceremony that is meaningful to them than others' (paras 1.33, 1.34). The consultation paper considers that there is no longer any 'policy justification for imposing such a patchwork of different rules on communities and couples' (para 7.15). It therefore proposes a new legal framework giving 'couples more freedom and flexibility over their wedding itself' and suggests that this liberalisation could be achieved by 'providing a robust system of preliminaries, to provide ample opportunity for impediments to be discovered, and forced and sham marriages to be identified' (para 1.92).

The proposed system shifts 'much of the focus of regulation onto the preliminaries stage' so 'that, with robust preliminaries to protect the interest of the state, the law could give couples more choice about the wedding ceremony itself' (para 3.7). Each person would need to give at least 28 days' notice and this would take the form of two steps: '(1) the initial giving of notice, which might take place remotely (for example, by post or online); and (2) an in-person meeting with a registration officer' (paras 3.11, 3.12). These steps could be taken at the same time or separately (para 3.13). The consultation paper asks whether these preliminaries should apply to Church of England and Church in Wales weddings, which would mean that the current Anglican preliminaries such as the calling of banns would no longer have legal effect (para 3.23).

The introduction of robust civil preliminaries which would apply across the board, with the possible exception of the Church of England/Church in Wales, would mean that the law on the wedding ceremony itself can be liberalised. Fairness and equality concerns also dictate that the separate treatment of different weddings in the current law should be eliminated in order 'to find rules that would work for all weddings' (para

1.96). The Law Commission propose that all weddings would be required to take place in the presence of an authorised 'officiant' (para 3.29). The term 'officiant' is used to denote 'the person who is responsible for ensuring that the legal requirements of the ceremony are met' (para 5.2). The officiant need not be the person who conducts or leads the ceremony, often referred to as the celebrant (para 3.31). The two roles may be performed by the same person or by different people (para 5.3). It is noted that 'separating out the roles helps to make it clear what is a matter for the law and what is a matter for religion, custom, practice, or personal choice'. Moreover, there are 'good reasons' why legislation should be 'generally silent on who should conduct the ceremony', given religious diversity: in a number of religious traditions, no third person is required to conduct the ceremony as such (paras 5.4, 5.6).

The Law Commission considers that 'the state's interest in marriage would be protected by making it clear that every ceremony should be attended by an officiant who had specific duties to ensure that the legal requirements were met, along with the responsibility to uphold the dignity and solemnity of marriage'. This would include '(1) ensuring that the couple freely consent to the marriage; (2) ensuring that any requirements of the ceremony have been met; and (3) ensuring that the register (or schedule) is signed' (paras 5.51–5.52). The liberalisation of the law on requirements as to ceremony would remove the 'existing requirement for open doors that applies to some types of wedding' (para 1.96). The location would 'be subject to the officiant's consent', with officiants being 'responsible for considering safety and dignity, with guidance on how to do so from the General Register Office' (para 3.66). The possibility of 'an optional scheme for pre-approval' would also be considered so that 'some venues would already have been determined to be safe and dignified, removing any need for an officiant to make their own assessment'.

It is proposed that 'all weddings should take place according to the form and ceremony chosen by the parties, and agreed by the officiant' (para 1.96). The main requirement would be that 'the parties should be required to express their consent to be married'. However, even here 'no specific form of words should be required' and 'consent should be able to be conveyed non-orally, for example by participating in a ritual according to religious rites'. The 'one exception' to the permissive rule allowing couples and officiants to determine the content of their own ceremonies is that 'although religious content would be permitted during civil ceremonies, the ceremony would be required to be identifiable as a civil ceremony rather than a religious service' (para 3.60). The paper considers that the 'the sharp distinction between civil and religious weddings' in the current law 'does not accommodate couples who have different beliefs, including couples made up of persons of different faiths, and couples in which one person is religious and the other is not' (para 1.38). It notes that, although civil registrars in the majority of cases 'wish to give couples a mean-ingful wedding, and so they accommodate couples' wishes to personalise their ceremonies', there is some evidence that some 'registration officers are taking a restrictive view as to what they allow couples to include as part of their wedding ceremony' (paras 6.15, 6.16).[2] The paper notes that the prohibition on 'including anything other than incidental religious content in their civil wedding ceremonies' is 'subject to interpretation, and so variable application, with content from some religions more likely to be excluded than others', therefore imposing 'an unnecessarily difficult burden on registration officers, who are tasked with trying to police an unclear rule' (para 6.73). It is proposed that 'the law should only prohibit religious service to the degree necessary to ensure that a civil wedding remains identifiable as a civil ceremony, and could not be mistaken for

---

[2] This draws on Stephanie Pywell and Rebecca Probert, 'Neither Sacred nor Profane: The Permitted Content of Civil Marriage Ceremonies' [2018] *Child and Family Law Quarterly* 415.

a religious wedding service' (para 6.106). This would mean that 'religious content should be permitted in civil wedding ceremonies, provided that the ceremony remains identifiable as a civil ceremony rather than a religious service (para 6.109). This objective, though laudable, might be difficult to define in practice.

These changes would mitigate the issue of unregistered religious marriages to the extent that the problem is caused by the current restrictions requiring a registered place of worship. The Law Commission's proposals would also go some way to resolving issues concerning non-religious marriages by adopting what they refer to as a scheme 'based on the regulation of officiants, rather than the regulation of the locations where weddings can take place' (para 1.92) and would facilitate non-religious belief weddings on an equal basis to religious ones.

An officiant-focused system

As noted earlier, under the Law Commission's schema, an officiant would be present at all weddings, 'with the law prescribing their role and responsibilities' (para 3.27). The paper explores the categories of person who could act as officiants (para 3.27) and, in so doing, provides a basis for non-religious marriages to have legal effect. Noting that their terms of reference requires them to 'consider how the law could be reformed to incorporate two new categories of officiants, if Government decides to enable either or both groups to solemnize marriages: officiants appointed by non-religious belief organisations and independent officiants' (para 3.35), the Law Commission proposes a schema that deals with non-religious belief organisations (such as humanists) and independent celebrants differently. This separate treatment, caused by the terms of reference, is one of the major flaws in the Law Commission's schema alongside the fact that, although Law Commission emphasises that its system is focused on the officiant, it is actually for the main part an organisation-focused approach. These criticisms will become clearer in our discussion of the Law Commission's categories of officiants. Their consultation paper proposes that 'officiants would fall into four, or possibly five, categories' (para 3.36).

Registration officers

The proposal that all marriages would be attended by one officiant would include civil weddings, where at the moment both a Superintendent Registrar and a Registrar are required to attend (paras 5.60–5.61). Registration officers would continue to officiate at civil weddings but, under the proposals, only one would need to attend, not two. These would continue to be appointed and employed by local authorities (paras 3.37 and 5.68). However, in order to combat existing confusion, given the anomaly of civil registrars being present at religious weddings and as a result of the proposal to permit religious weddings to take place in a wider range of locations, it is proposed that 'registrars would only be able to officiate at civil weddings, not at religious weddings' (para 5.57). This, however, sits oddly with the Law Commission's proposed relaxation of the rules on religious content. It would mean that 'religious groups would need to ensure that a religious officiant was present instead (para 5.59)'.

Anglican clergy

Clerks in Holy Orders within the Church of England and the Church in Wales would be recognised as officiants by virtue of their office. The Law Commission states that 'they would be authorised by virtue of their ordination, by being in Holy Orders' (para 3.38). This is in line with the Marriage Act 1949, which reflects their position under ecclesiastical law rather than conferring the authority (para 5.76). The paper notes that both the Church of England and the Church in Wales 'have generally accepted duties to conduct the weddings of their parishioners when called upon to do so', and this merits special treatment (para 5.77). The paper also points to the formal process of ordination and the internal discipline in those churches and states that, in contrast, 'within many religious traditions the question of who conducts a wedding is far more fluid' (para 5.84). However, this misses the point slightly: the difference is that in respect of the Church of England its processes of appointment and discipline are part of the law of the land. This leaves the Church in Wales in a slightly odd position: its differential treatment is legally justified on the basis that its general processes of appointment and discipline were formerly part of the law of the land but its specific role in relation to marriage has been preserved.

Nominated officiants

In contrast, all other religious marriages would fall under the third category on the basis that where the religious body does not have a special legal status then 'the recognition of other religious officiants usually requires a nomination'. The Law Commission proposes that the relevant governing authority of all other religious groups should be able to nominate officiants to the General Register Office (para 5.97). The Law Commission's paper leaves open for discussion whether nominating bodies could 'nominate persons by the office that they hold within the organisation' rather than just nominating individuals (para 3.46). The General Register Office would be responsible for keeping a publicly available list of all nominated officiants (para 3.41).

The Law Commission have taken the view that 'if Government determined that non-religious groups should be able to solemnize weddings, non-religious belief organisations would be able to nominate officiants in the same way as religious groups' (paras 3.39–3.40). They note that since, in order to be eligible to nominate, 'a religious organisation would have to fall within the description of a religious body given by the Supreme Court in *Hodkin*',[3] then a similar definition should apply to non-religious belief organisations (para 3.2). According to paragraph 57 of Lord Toulson's judgment in *Hodkin*, religion can be described in summary as 'a spiritual or non-secular belief system, held by a group of adherents, which claims to explain mankind's place in the universe and relationship with the infinite, and to teach its adherents how they are to live their lives in conformity with the spiritual understanding associated with the belief system'. The Law Commission's proposed definition of non-religious belief organisation is: 'An organisation that professes a secular belief system that claims to explain humanity's nature and relationship to the universe, and to teach its adherents how they are to live their lives in conformity with the understanding associated with the belief system' (para 3.43).

This parasitical use of the *Hodkin* definition is problematic in that not all non-religious belief systems may be 'secular', either in the common use of the word or in the sense it was used in *Hodkin*. Lord Toulson went on to say that 'by spiritual or non-secular I mean a belief system which goes beyond that which can be perceived by the senses or ascertained by the application of science'. Moreover, this parasitical definition tells us very little. It is a functional definition which reveals even less than the human rights and discrimination law jurisprudence on the definition of belief. The existing definition found in section 14 of the Marriage (Same Sex Couples) Act 2013 (which speaks of 'an organisation whose principal or sole purpose is the advancement of a system of non-religious beliefs which relate to morality or ethics') would be preferable. It is noteworthy that, despite adapting the *Hodkin* definition, the Law Commission accepts that it is not sufficient and notes that it would need to be considered 'whether the definition

---

[3]   *R (on the Application of Hodkin) v Registrar General of Births, Deaths and Marriages* [2013] UKSC 77.

of a non-religious belief organisation should be limited further, by a list of exclusions of the types of group that would not qualify to nominate officiants, such as political parties, trade unions, or sporting organisations' (para 3.43) Similar issues have developed in the discrimination law case law and the definition found in section 14 of the 2013 Act would go some way to resolving them. Although the Law Commission's terms of reference state that they are bound by the definition of religion in *Hodkin*, this does not mean that it should be the basis for defining non-religious beliefs.

The Law Commission proposes that for both religious and non-religious organisations alike there should be three further requirements (para 3.44). Notably these requirements do not relate to buildings. The paper notes that given, that their proposed scheme envisages moving away from requiring weddings to take place in particular locations, 'it would be anomalous to require a religious group to have a registered place of worship in order to appoint an officiant' (paras 5.70, 5.71).

The first requirement is that there are 'at least 20 members who meet regularly for worship or in furtherance of their beliefs'. This figure of 20 has been suggested because, although it 'might seem like a relatively low threshold, … this has been the minimum figure for registering a place of worship for weddings for over 180 years without, as far as we know, causing any problems' (para 5.97). However, this requirement may not be appropriate for small groups or religions and belief systems who do not gather communally. The paper circumvents this by suggesting that a relaxed approach should be taken to its interpretation. It notes that this requirement 'will not pose problems for interfaith ministry groups' because, although they 'do not generally hold large religious services for the public', their members communicate among themselves regularly and they provide pastoral care and so there are 'meetings to plan and provide support to one another in how they engage with the community and meetings in furtherance of their religious beliefs' (para 5.98). It is even suggested that this 'requirement could be satisfied by remote meetings amongst celebrants or the executive of the organisation in relation to community outreach and training of celebrants' (para 5.131). These examples show the inadequacy of this requirement. Insisting instead that the organisation has existed for a certain number of years, as many of the amendments and proposals discussed in the last chapter did, or saying that the existence of a building could be one ground upon which the requirement would be met, would be a conservative approach but one that would be more appropriate.

The second requirement is that the organisation should have 'a wedding service or a sincerely held belief about marriage' (para 3.44). The purpose of this rule is to 'help to limit the power to nominate officiants to those groups that would genuinely intend to officiate at weddings' (para 5.99). It is unclear what the words 'genuinely intend' mean here; perhaps it is a reference to excluding sham marriages.[4] But it is questionable whether sham marriages can be policed in this way, given that the requirement would 'not be seen as any form of check by the state on the content of the ceremony' and would not stipulate that 'the precise terms of that wedding service should have to be used in every case'. This would be an ineffective way of avoiding sham marriages, given that there would invariably be some form of marriage service once officiants are appointed. Focusing on an organisation's beliefs about marriage seems to be an unnecessary and inappropriate imposition which

---

[4] A 'sham marriage' is defined under section 24 of the Immigration Act 1999 as existing where either or both parties are not a national citizen, where there is no genuine relationship between them and where they enter into the marriage to avoid the effect of immigration law or the immigration rules and/or to obtain a right conferred by that law or those rules. It does not matter whether or not the marriage is void. Section 24 imposes a duty on registrars to report suspicious marriages, which section 24A extends to suspicious civil partnerships.

goes against the Law Commission's insistence that the focus is now on officiants, not organisations: determining whether an organisation has a belief about marriage could require the General Register Office to get into theological and doctrinal issues.

The third requirement is that the Law Commission will consider 'whether there should be an express exclusion preventing organisations from nominating officiants if the organisation promotes purposes that are unlawful or contrary to public policy or morality' (para 3.44). The paper notes that 'while there is no specific exclusion of such groups under the current law, we understand that the General Register Office takes the view that it would be able to refuse to register the buildings of such groups for weddings, in the event that any applied' (para 5.100). It is unclear why this would need to be explicitly laid out in the case of bodies nominating individuals rather than bodies registering buildings. Making such an imposition again suggests that the Law Commission's schema is focused on organisations rather than officiants.

These requirements show the inadequacy of the definition of belief provided and risk providing a very low threshold for what would constitute a religion or belief. The inadequate definition of belief and the low threshold imposed would also open the floodgates. The definition already found in section 14 of the Marriage (Same Sex Couples) Act 2013 would be preferable and would provide some protection against beliefs being created solely in order to be included under the legislation. Alternatively, it may be questioned why nominating organisations should be limited to religion or belief organisations. The terms of reference discouraged the Law Commission from engaging with this question: they were tasked to create a system which could include non-religious belief and independent-celebrant ceremonies, and so did not consider why the line should be drawn there and the merits of a more expansive scheme.

Independent officiants

The Law Commission proposes a fourth category which would include independent celebrants (if the government decided to enable them to solemnise marriages). Individuals would be able to apply to the General Register Office for authorisation and the General Register Office would be responsible for keeping a list of all independent officiants (para 3.50). Like all other officiants, independent officiants would need to prove that they were a 'fit and proper person', would need to have undertaken relevant training and would need to undertake ongoing training (paras 5.166, 3.51 and 3.52). The difference would be that while the training for nominated officiants could take place in a number of ways and could be internal to their nominating body (paras 3.47–3.48), for independent officiants training would be either provided by the General Register Office or approved by the Registrar General (paras 3.51–3.52).

Depending on how strict these requirements are and how they are enforced they could either place a significant burden on registration officials or open the door to all kinds of celebrants, which would have the effect of making the third category redundant, on the basis that if anyone could apply to be an independent officiant then there is no reason to limit nominating organisations to religion or belief organisations. There is also the question of why independent celebrants cannot be covered by the third category. The Law Commission rules this out simply on the basis that they 'are not aware of any jurisdiction in which celebrants can be nominated by a body that is neither a religious organisation nor a non-religious belief organisation' (para 5.139). The Law Commission concluded that:

> While there are organisations such as the Wedding Celebrancy Commission that could potentially act as a nominating body, allowing an organisation that was not a religious or belief organisation to nominate officiants would undermine the very point of having definitions

of religion or belief and detract from the recognition of those organisations. In addition, not all independent celebrants are affiliated to an organisation, and it might be a contradiction in terms to require an 'independent' celebrant to be a part of an organisation.

The first reason given is diluted, however, by the inadequacy of the definitions of religion or belief discussed earlier. Given the difficulties of defining religion or belief, it may be preferable to open the definition to all organisations. Recognising independent celebrants without such celebrants even being a member of an organisation will already cross this line. Individuals will be able to solemnise marriages who are neither State employees nor representatives of religion or belief organisations. The Law Commission's fourth category is a pure example of an officiant-focused approach and it leaves the third category looking quaint by comparison. It is likely that this fourth category will prove to be very popular. Indeed, if independent celebrants can go straight to the General Register Office, then it could be asked, why should religion or belief officiants be denied that opportunity and be required to operate through their organisation and so be subject to further regulation concerning their organisation rather than themselves? Why should a religious leader of a faith of just 19 members be denied the right to solemnise marriages while an independent celebrant who represents just themselves has that power?

In relation to the second reason for the need for a separate approach for independent celebrants (that some independent celebrants are truly independent), the paper does consider whether independent celebrants should be members of a professional organisation providing insurance or whether they should be required to take out insurance. It concludes that while being a member of a recognised trade body should not be a legal requirement, it 'may help officiants to access the necessary training and continuing professional development' (para 5.170). Similarly, it concludes that taking out individual insurance should not be a prerequisite but that 'it seems a matter of good practice and professionalism to obtain such insurance' (paras 5.171, 5.172). The fact that both the Association of Independent Celebrants and the Wedding Celebrancy Commission have such requirements suggests that there may be more scope for independent officiants to fall under the third heading, provided that nominated officiants are not limited only to religion or belief organisations. Indeed, if independent celebrants fell under the third heading then concerns about individual insurance would not arise and so it would be preferable for independent celebrants who are members of umbrella organisations to apply through their organisations. Stephanie Pywell's empirical research found that only 14% of her respondents were not members of a larger group.[5] However, this is likely to be an underestimate of the number of truly independent celebrants, given her method-ology which used the umbrella organisations as the point of contact (with one exception). It follows that there will be a minority of independent celebrants who do not belong to an umbrella organisation who could serve as the nominating body for the purpose of the third type of officiant. However, the lack of supervision might give reason not to include them. Even if they are to be included, that does not preclude the majority of independent celebrants being included under the third rather than fourth type of officiant, which would bolster the role of the umbrella organisation and reduce the burden and discretion placed upon the General Register Office or Registrar General. Indeed, the proposal to relax the rule on the use of religious content at civil weddings is likely to have the effect of reducing the number of independent-celebrant

---

[5] Stephanie Pywell, 'The Day of their Dreams: Celebrant-Led Wedding Celebration Ceremonies' [2020] *Child and Family Law Quarterly* 177; Stephanie Pywell, 'Beyond Beliefs: A Proposal to give Couples in England and Wales a Real Choice of Marriage Officiants' [2020] *Child and Family Law Quarterly* 215.

ceremonies on the basis that Pywell's research suggests that their popularity arises from the way in which they alone at the moment can blend religious and non-religious content.

Maritime officiants

The fifth category need not concern us here.[6]

The Law Commission's promotion of the officiant-focused system is radical, in that it represents a clear move away from a building-based approach and tries to provide a focus that unites the different ways of getting married. However, perhaps what is proposed is too radical for it to be politically possible, in that it requires a completely different approach that would affect all religious bodies other than the Church of England/Church in Wales, who in many cases have conducted weddings for hundreds of years. The officiant focus is also blurred at times: it does not really apply to the Church of England/Church in Wales marriages where couples are opting to marry in the parish church rather than choosing the cleric, and this may also be true of other religious marriages: the building focus of the current law is discriminatory, but many who choose a religious wedding choose that because of the venue, not the person. The Law Commission's idea that there needs to be an officiant is sound, but the system does not need to be officiant focused. Indeed, what is proposed is not really officiant focused at all. With the exception of the fourth category, the focus is more on organisations than individuals.

Mitigating the problem of unregistered marriages

The proposals discussed earlier deal with the issue of non-religious marriage and would make a significant difference

---

[6] See para 3.54–3.56.

to the unregistered religious marriages issue by removing the requirements as to where and how marriages can take place that indirectly discriminate against religions who either do not have places of worship or have a tradition of marriage ceremonies taking place elsewhere. As the Law Commission's consultation paper puts it, their proposals 'should make it easier to have a religious wedding that is also a legally binding wedding' (para 10.180). However, with respect to what the Law Commission styles as 'religious only weddings' (para 10.8), the consultation paper noted that some mitigation might be achieved through revision of the law of validity and through criminal offences.

The law on validity

Although the Court of Appeal in *Attorney General v Akhter* expressed 'doubt whether it is possible or, indeed, sensible to set out precisely when a marriage would be regarded as falling within the Marriage Act 1949',[7] the Law Commission proposes doing exactly that on the basis that this will provide greater clarity, which should reduce 'the scope for accidental non-compliance' (paras 10.106, 10.107). The Law Commission proposes that an opposite-sex marriage would be valid 'as long as the couple have given notice, and at least one of them believes that the person officiating at the ceremony is authorised to solemnize a legal marriage'. This focuses on 'what was known to the couple, rather than whether as a matter of fact the person officiating was authorised to do so', because 'whether the person officiating has the authority to do so is not necessarily within the couple's knowledge' (para 10.73).

However, it is noticeable that while both parties need to give notice, only one of them needs to believe that there is an authorised officiant (para 10.55). This would mean that the marriage is still valid if only one of the couple knows that

---

[7] *Her Majesty's Attorney General v Akhter* [2020] EWCA Civ 122, para 66.

the officiant is not authorised. The purpose is to protect the party who was unaware and, by making the marriage valid, this rule would have the effect of frustrating the plan of the person who seeks to dupe the other into an unregistered marriage. It is difficult, however, to see why such a marriage should be valid rather than void or voidable. That would protect the unaware party, while at the same time making it clear that a marriage where one party knows that the officiant is not authorised is not a valid marriage because, as we have seen, parties to a void marriage have the same access to divorce law in the case of relationship breakdown as those who are in a valid marriage.

Under the Law Commission's schema, an opposite-sex marriage would be declared void where notice has not been given by both or either party or if the parties both know that the officiant is not authorised (or there is no officiant). This would mean that financial remedies available on divorce can be applied. (para 10.128). There would be a non-qualifying opposite-sex wedding, and therefore no legal redress, where (a) one or both parties do not consent or (b) the couple have not given notice *and* (i) they both know that the officiant is not authorised or (ii) there is no officiant at all (paras 10.109 and 10.130). The paper states that 'this would go a long way towards addressing the key problem of religious-only marriages, where some individuals do not realise what is required and are left without any remedy at the end of a lengthy relationship' (para 10.63). There is no doubt, however, that the system put forward by the Law Commission continues to be complex, as shown by the fact that they seek to explain it using both a table and a diagram.[8] However, an alternative way of conceptualising their proposals would be to say that the status of the marriage depends on the answers to three questions: (1) Have both parties given notice? (2) Have both parties given consent?

---

[8]   Para 10.127 and Appendix 6.

Table 6.1: Law Commission's proposals on validity

(1) Have both parties given notice?	(2) Have both parties given consent?	(3) Do both or one of the parties believe that the officiant is authorised?	What is the status of the opposite-sex marriage?
Yes	Yes	Yes	Valid
No	Yes	Yes	Void
Yes	Yes	No	Void
Yes	Yes but vitiated by duress, mistake, impaired mental capacity or similar other factors	Yes	Voidable
Yes	No	Yes	Non-qualifying
No	Yes	No	Non-qualifying
No	No	No	Non-qualifying

(3) Do both or one of the parties believe that the officiant is authorised? Adopting that framework, the proposals could be summarised as shown in Table 6.1.

It is noticeable, however, that this would have made no direct difference to the outcome of *Akhter v Khan*.[9] If the underlying principle is that unregistered marriages are of concern where there has not been a free and informed choice to opt out of legal protection, then the Law Commission's proposals will not go far enough. Their proposals mean that those who believe that the person officiating at the ceremony is authorised to solemnise a legal marriage will have a void marriage and be

---

9   [2018] EWFC 54.

entitled to legal redress, but this will not apply to those who have been promised a legally binding ceremony at some point (the *Akhter v Khan* situation) or where one party has been put under pressure by the other party not to have a legally binding ceremony. The current position that a marriage would be voidable where consent had been vitiated by duress, mistake, impaired mental capacity or similar other factors would remain unchanged but might not cover these situations (and did not cover the situation in *Akhter v Khan*).

Criminal offences

In terms of proposing offences, the Law Commission's paper notes that the government has committed to responding to the Independent Review into the Application of Sharia Law in England and Wales and, since this work is being taken forward separately to the Law Commission's review, the paper will 'therefore not consider the creation of a new offence along the lines suggested in the Independent Sharia Review as part of its work' (para 1.80). That said, the Law Commission does make a provisional proposal in relation to offences and this follows the Independent Review in focusing on the person conducting the ceremony. When read in the context of the consultation paper as a whole, it is clear that this criminal offence proposal is a backstop which would simply prohibit officiants and pseudo-officiants from making misrepresentations. It would do nothing to give redress to the couple themselves. However, the risk in making such a recommendation is that the proposed criminal offence could be seen as a magic-bullet solution (as the Independent Review and others saw similar offences). That is not what the Law Commission is proposing, but on a glance of their proposals it is possible to erroneously assume this. It is vital that their proposed criminal offence is not seen in that way and not detached from the other proposals which will make much more of a difference.

The Law Commission notes that currently 'it is an offence for any person to solemnize a marriage according to Anglican rites falsely pretending to be in Holy Orders, but it is not an offence to pretend to be an authorised person or superintendent registrar' (para 10.144). They therefore propose that it should be an offence: '(1) for any person to purport to be an officiant and deliberately or recklessly mislead either of the couple about their status or the effect of the ceremony; or (2) for an officiant deliberately or recklessly to mislead either of the couple about the effect of the ceremony' (para 10.170). If the Law Commission's proposal to create the officiant role is taken up, then this offence makes some sense. Indeed, the Commission's general proposals help to remedy a major defect in the offence proposed by the Independent Review. As the paper notes, the Independent Review's proposed offence would be 'unlikely to be effective' under the current law, given that there is no legal requirement 'for an identified person to conduct a non-Anglican religious wedding – or indeed any person at all' (para 5.35). The Law Commission's creation of the legally responsible role of the officiant therefore provides a relevant person to whom criminal responsibility could apply. The Law Commission contends that their proposed offence would 'reduce the likelihood of either of the couple being misled as to the nature of the ceremony' and is 'intended to deter individuals from purporting to officiate at weddings when they are not authorised to do so' (para 10.188). These aims are laudable and logical in so far as the proposed offence removes a possible gap in the law. However, as will be discussed in Chapter Eight, it may be questioned whether general criminal offences such as those found in the Fraud Act 2006 already criminalise such behaviour.

Moreover, the reference to deterring individuals from purporting to officiate shows that this proposed offence suffers from the same defect as the offence suggested in the Independent Review. There is no evidence to suggest that the problem of unregistered religious marriages is mainly attributable to rogue officiants. Creating and clarifying the legal responsibilities of officiants, as the Law Commission suggests, will help to mitigate the number of unregistered religious marriages and will, arguably, do enough to get any rogue officiants in line without the threat of criminal sanction. Such a possibility of criminal sanction will in any event have a limited effect on the problem of unregistered religious marriages.

The Law Commission consultation paper presents both sets of changes as having a limited effect: the law of validity is described as a 'blunt instrument' (para 10.201), while criminal sanctions are dismissed as 'blunt tool' (para 10.153). The paper generally concedes that there are 'limits to our reforms' and that some religious weddings will continue to be classed as 'non-qualifying' (para 10.190). The paper rejected 'automatically treat[ing] all religious weddings or particular types of religious weddings as legal weddings', noting that 'holding that a simple exchange of consent could generate legal consequences would also risk deregulating marriage entirely' (paras 10.196, 10.197). Similarly, the Law Commission does not propose attaching 'legal consequences to such ceremonies in and of themselves' (para 10.190).[10] It notes that some couples may wish to have unregistered marriages:

> A number of our stakeholders told us that some couples might want to make a statement of their commitment to each other without expressing their consent to be legally married. Humanists UK has cautiously estimated that around 20% of couples who have a Humanist ceremony may not have a legally binding marriage ceremony as well. The Pagan Federation, in its 13th programme consultation response, noted that some couples will not necessarily want a legal ceremony, or to have the 'terms

---

[10] Cf. John Eekelaar, 'Marriage: A Modest Proposal' [2013] *Family Law* 83.

of such a relationship … determined by the civil law'. The Board of Deputies similarly told us that some Jewish couples currently opt for religious-only weddings. (para 10.89)

This underlines the extent to which the unregistered religious (or belief) marriage phenomenon is not limited to Islam and, given the lack of research on this point, it would be useful if the Law Commission were to publish the information on this that it has been given. Moreover, this underlines that it should not be a question of eliminating unregistered religious marriages per se. The paper further points out that, although there 'are cases where a legal remedy would be appropriate, the need for a remedy in these cases derives from what has happened during the relationship rather than the ceremony itself, and so falls outside the scope of what can be achieved by reform to weddings law' (para 10.190). The paper notes Barlow and Smithson's research, which shows that that these issues arose too in relation to cohabitants (para 10.201).[11] For the Law Commission, this suggests that 'the correct approach in such cases is to focus on the consequences of the relationship coming to an end, rather than on the ceremony' (para 10.204). The Law Commission therefore repeated its previous call for reform of the law of cohabitation rights,[12] noting that 'reform of the law relating to cohabitation would be able to ensure protection of those whose religious ceremonies have no legal consequences' in a way that focuses 'on the relationship in a way that weddings law cannot' (para 10.205).

---

[11] Anne Barlow and Janet Smithson, 'Legal Assumptions, Cohabitants' Talk and the Rocky Road to Reform' (2010) 22 (3) *Child and Family Law Quarterly* 328.

[12] Law Commission, *Cohabitation: The Financial Consequences of Relationship Breakdown* (Law Com No 307, 2007).

Conclusion

The Law Commission will publish its final report on weddings law reform in late 2021 and it will then be considered by the government. Few Law Commission reports result in legislation and, even where they do, they are often significantly amended as part of the parliamentary process. It would be unfortunate if the Law Commission's proposals were not taken forward by the government, however, especially given the decision in *R (On Application of Harrison) v Secretary of State for Justice*.[13] Although this chapter has expressed concern at the details, especially concerning the definition of belief, whether organisations other than religious or belief organisations should be included and whether the differential treatment of independent celebrants is sound, the Law Commission's radical and comprehensive proposals would provide a solution to the concerns expressed about the current non-recognition of non-religious marriages. The general direction of travel proposed and the changes to preliminaries, ceremony and location are sound and much needed.

These proposals would also have a significant effect upon decreasing the number of unregistered religious marriages. This is mostly through the shift away from the focus on buildings, which indirectly discriminates against some religious traditions. The proposed changes as to validity, though still perhaps overly complex, would also help to deal with the issue by increasing the circumstances where weddings that are not legally recognised will be void rather than non-qualifying, with the result that financial relief can be then provided on the breakdown. The proposed criminal offence would support and enhance the officiant focus but would do little to redress the problem of unregistered religious marriages. Overall, the Law Commission's proposals do not provide a singular magic-bullet

---

[13] [2020] EWHC 2096 (Admin).

solution but a number of changes which individually and cumulatively would provide a significant degree of mitigation of the problem. It will therefore be vital that their proposals are not interpreted as a menu of options to cherry-pick from. The consultation paper could be clearer in underlining this, but it does recognise that the proposals suggested will mitigate rather than solve the unregistered marriage issue.

It is clear, however, that, despite their strengths, the Law Commission's proposals will not be sufficient. The next part will explore a package of reforms could be developed that could deal with the issues concerning religion and marriage law identified so far. The chapters that follow will draw upon and develop the Law Commission's proposals to develop a comprehensive system of reforms which could be enacted through a new Act of Parliament – say, an Intimate Adult Relationships Act – which could provide an equal, fair and modernised law recognising and regulating intimate adult relationships.

PART III

Reform Proposals

SEVEN

Reforming Weddings Law

Introduction

This chapter turns to the question of reform, proposing specific reform proposals showing in detail how the consolidation, simplification and modernisation of the law on intimate adult relationships should be achieved. These will rest on our two points of principle. The first is that the legal redress should be provided to those in unregistered religious marriages where the failure to comply with registration requirements is unwitting or is not truly voluntary by one of the parties. The second is that non-religious ceremonies including those conducted by independent celebrants should be legally binding.

Outline of the reforms needed

The Law Commission's proposals, examined in the last chapter, would mark an important step forward but would not be sufficient, for two reasons: first, the Law Commission is hampered by its terms of reference, meaning that, as it concedes, it can only mitigate the unregistered marriage issue; second, there are a few shortcomings in what the Law Commission proposes, especially in relation to the definition of belief systems and the fact that independent celebrants are treated differently. This means that the Law Commission's proposals will not completely fulfil either of the two points of principle. Moreover, there is a significant risk that the Law Commission's recommendations may be cherry-picked by the government rather than enacted in full. This would be disastrous, given that the strength of the Law Commission's proposals is that they come as a complete package.

The reform proposals discussed in this section also come as a complete package. They develop and refine the Law Commission's proposals, drawing upon comparative examples. However, they go further than the Law Commission's terms of reference. The focus needs to be not just on weddings law reform or even marriage law but on the law regulating intimate adult relationships. There needs to be a new statute – say, an Intimate Adult Relationships Act – which would consolidate and modernise the law on marriage and civil partnerships for both opposite- and same-sex couples, as well as introducing certain rights for cohabiting couples. This would replace existing restrictive rules that indirectly discriminate against some religious traditions which exclude non-religious cere- monies and ceremonies conducted by independent celebrants and which provide virtually no rights for cohabitees on rela- tionship breakdown.

This section will outline the main changes that need to be made and, where appropriate, will show how this change could be drafted in legislation. In sum, there are six changes that need to be made.

(i) As suggested by the Law Commission, an officiant must be in attendance at all weddings. They need not necessarily be the celebrant but the officiant would be responsible for ensuring that the legal requirements are met and will be required to have undergone and to undergo regular training.

(ii) Unlike the Law Commission's proposals, officiants in the future would be appointed in one of two ways: by a nominating organisation or by individual application. The nominating organisation would not be limited to religion or belief organisations and would therefore also include umbrella organisations of independent celebrants and, indeed, any other organisation that wished to solemnise marriages. Continuity provisions would ensure that civil registrars and those who represent religions that already solemnise marriages would be automatically included subject to requirements for ongoing training. Existing provisions concerning religious same-sex marriages would continue to apply. Individual application would be exceptional and would apply only where the officiant is not a member of any organisation.

(iii) The Law Commission's proposals in terms of common preliminaries and the importance of giving notice would be adopted in full, allowing for complete liberalisation of how and where marriages can take place. Stringent rules on preliminaries would allow a uniform and otherwise minimal law on marriage. Decisions as to form and location would be a matter for the officiant, who would be bound by the rules of their nominating organisation. However, there would be a requirement for both of the parties to express their consent.

(iv) The law on validity would be codified and simplified to require three elements for a valid marriage. A valid marriage would exist where both of the parties (1) give notice before the wedding, (2) believe that there is an authorised officiant at the wedding and (3) express consent at the wedding. A void marriage would exist where either (1) or (2) have not been met but the other two requirements have been met. A non-qualifying marriage will exist where (3) is not met and/or where both (1) and (2) have not been met. A marriage will be voidable where the consent is vitiated by duress, mistake, impaired mental capacity or similar other factors.

(v) Existing criminal offences on forced marriage, coercive control and fraud would be amended to ensure that they explicitly cover the situation (a) where the defendant forces or coerces the victim to enter into a non-qualifying marriage, (b) where the defendant either is an officiant or purports to be an officiant and dishonestly makes a false representation as to the status or the effect of the ceremony, intending to make a gain for himself or another, or to cause loss to another or to expose another to a risk of loss.

(vi) Limited and specific rights on separation for those who cohabit would be introduced, focused on redressing advantages gained and disadvantages suffered as a result of the relationship, with opt-out provisions ensuring free choice is respected.

The first three changes would bring about a modernised, equal and clear law on weddings. This chapter will focus on the first three proposals. The last three changes provide backstop provisions concerning other areas of law that would support these changes, helping to mitigate further inequalities that can occur as a result of unregistered religious marriages. These will be discussed in the next two chapters. Given that of these three backstop provisions, the last would be the most effective, a separate chapter will be dedicated to the issue of cohabitation reform.

It is clear that the Marriage Act 1949 is no longer fit for purpose. The current system is a throwback to a bygone age. In particular, the current law is in need of reform given that the requirements it makes are not applied equally, indirectly discriminate against some religious traditions and exclude a number of marriage ceremonies that are now common, namely those conducted by independent celebrants and humanist and other belief organisations. The current law fails to fulfil its purpose: there is now often confusion as to who is married. Many couples who go through a religious, belief or independent celebrant ceremony think that they are married, or at least use that language. The myth of common law marriage casts a long shadow, with it also being commonly but erroneously believed that living together over a period of time means that redress would be provided on relationship breakdown. In some respects, we are back in the very position that the Marriage Act 1753 sought to deal with: the serious and prevalent problem of marriages being conducted in various and unusual ways of which the State is largely ignorant.

Significant reform of the law of marriage is desperately needed and many of the recommendations in the Law Commission's consultation paper would fulfil this need. The emphasis upon the importance of preliminaries and the Law Commission's suggestions as to the modernisation of the process is sound. This would facilitate a minimalistic law on where and how marriages take place which would allow couples to personalise their cere-monies. This would also have the effect of mitigating the problem of unregistered marriages by removing obstacles that are currently in the way of those who seek a legally recognised marriage but are frustrated by the requirements of the Marriage Act 1949. The cre-ation of the position of officiant and the focus on stringent rules as to preliminaries would enable equal and minimalistic regulation of where and how weddings take place. The creation of the pos-ition of officiant (who must be in attendance at all weddings but need not necessarily be the celebrant) would be an important step forward, providing a person to whom legal duties and responsi-bilities can be attached while recognising that marriages will be solemnised in different traditions in different ways. This chapter will say nothing more about the Law Commission's proposals that the reform suggestions here broadly support. Instead, it will focus on the second reform proposal listed earlier: the question of how officiants are appointed.

Comparative examples

In relation to the question of how officiants are appointed, the Law Commission consultation paper rightly rejects the current sole focus on registering buildings for religious weddings as being 'restrictive' and ineffective, noting that at best it can 'be seen as a proxy measure for its stability and status'.[1] It also states that 'no other jurisdiction that we are aware of requires an organisation to have a building as a precondition for conducting weddings'. As they note, there are three broad approaches that neighbouring jurisdictions take: 'recognising the office holders of specific groups as officiants', 'allowing certain types of groups to nominate officiants' or 'allowing individuals to apply to be authorised as officiants' (para 5.72). However, by looking closer at the laws in these jurisdictions, it becomes clear that it is rarely the case that any jurisdiction chooses just one of these approaches. This might suggest that what is required is a fusion of the different approaches and that the balance suggested by the Law Commission is questionable. Before outlining preferred reform options, it is therefore useful to explore the systems that are in operation in neighbouring jurisdictions.

Scotland[2]

According to the Law Commission, Scotland operates an 'organisational model' (para 1.56). The Marriage (Scotland) Act 1977 (as amended by the Marriage and Civil Partnership (Scotland) Act 2014) provides a system that registers celebrants, not buildings, but these celebrants must represent an organisation. Registrars must either be district or assistant registrars appointed by the Registrar General (section 17) or celebrants for religious or belief marriages. Under section 8, this second category includes three groups: ministers and deacons of the Church of Scotland (who are recognised by virtue of their office); celebrants recognised by a religion or belief body

---

[1] Law Commission, *Getting Married: A Consultation Paper on Weddings Law* (Consultation Paper 247, 2020) para 5.95.

[2] For fuller discussion of the Scottish position, see Murray McLean, 'Beyond Belief: The Law and Practice of Marriage Formation in Contemporary Scotland' [2018] *Child and Family Law Quarterly* 237.

which has been prescribed by regulation as being entitled to solemnise marriages; and those who are members of a religion or belief body who have been nominated to the Registrar General under section 9 or section 12 of the Act (which provides for temporary authorisation). The term 'religious or belief body' is defined under section 26 as 'an organised group of people which meets regularly for worship or the principal object (or one of the principal objects) of which is to uphold or promote philosophical beliefs and which meets regularly for that purpose'.

The Law Commission's paper is critical of this approach and the fact that some religion or belief groups are prescribed, on the basis that this 'would replicate many of the problems with prescribing the groups whose office holders could automatically officiate at weddings' and 'would also need to be a very long list, to avoid taking away the right to conduct weddings from groups that have long been able to do so'.[3] However, such a criticism may be hasty. There is a need for a continuity provision whereby those religious groups who already solemnise marriage can continue to do so without either being specifically prescribed in legislation (as under the Scottish model) or having to re-nominate all celebrants (under the Law Commission model).

Independent celebrants are excluded under the Scottish model, since they are not attached to a religion or belief organisation. Figures for 2019 indicate that there were 26,007 marriages in Scotland, with 12,635 civil ceremonies and 13,372 religion or belief ceremonies.[4] Of this latter category, 3,276 were conducted by the Humanist Society Scotland, 2,225 by the Church of Scotland and 1,270 are down as 'Independent

---

[3]   Law Commission, *Getting Married: A Consultation Paper on Weddings Law* (Consultation Paper 247, 2020) para 5.92.

[4]   National Records of Scotland, *Vital Events Reference Tables 2019*. Section 7: Marriages and Civil Partnerships, Table 7.07: 'Marriages, by denomination, Scotland, 2019'.

Humanist Ceremonies'. This might suggest that the failure to accommodate independent celebrants has led some to classify themselves as belief organisations. This suggests that not recognising independent celebrants will put pressure on the definition of belief.

Ireland[5]

By contrast, the Irish model has a nomination system which focuses on the definition of what they term 'a secular body'. The Civil Registration Act 2004 (as amended by the Civil Registration (Amendment) Act 2012) provides that 'a marriage may be solemnised by, and only by, a registered solemniser' and must take place in a place that is open to the public (section 51). A register of solemnisers is kept and solemnisers are registered only if the body concerned is a religious body or a secular body (section 53). Such bodies can apply for registration of persons who are aged 18 or more. Where one or more members are already registered then the body shall not make a further application unless they are satisfied that there is a need for a larger number of its members to be so registered (section 54). A temporary authorisation may also be given under section 57.

'Secular body' is defined in section 45A as 'an organised group of people' which 'has not fewer than 50 members', where 'its principal objects are secular, ethical and humanist', its members 'meet regularly in relation to their beliefs', which does not have rules regarding marriage that contravene the law, has been in existence for a continuous period of not less than five years, 'does not having making a profit as one of its principal objects' and maintains a register of its members. The body must satisfy the authorities that it 'has appropriate

---

[5] For further discussion of the Irish legislation see Susan Leahy and Kathryn O'Sullivan, 'Changing Conceptions of Marriage in Ireland: Law and Practice' [2018] *Child and Family Law Quarterly* 279.

procedures in writing for selecting, training and accrediting members as fit and proper persons to solemnise marriages'. Political parties, bodies that promote a political party, bodies that promote a political cause, trade unions and chambers of commerce are all excluded from the definition, as are any bodies that promote purposes that are unlawful, contrary to public morality or policy, support terrorism or are for the benefit of an organisation membership of which is unlawful. This provides a useful template of how a non-religious belief category could be defined, but, like the Scottish model, the lack of explicit recognition for independent celebrants runs the risk that the secular category will be used to allow recognition of some but not all such ceremonies in an unprincipled way.

Northern Ireland[6]

Under Article 9 of the Marriage (Northern Ireland) Order 2003, religious marriages can be solemnised only by an officiant, while civil marriages are those solemnised by a person appointed under Article 31. Under Article 10, a religious body may apply to the Registrar General for a member named in the application who is aged 21 or over to be registered as an officiant. Article 2 defines a 'religious body' as 'an organised group of people meeting regularly for common religious worship', while Article 11 states that the Registrar General shall keep a register of persons registered to solemnise marriages in Northern Ireland. Temporary authorisation is provided under Article 14. The Article 31 system for civil weddings permits a local registration authority, with the approval of the Registrar General, to appoint a registrar of marriages and one or more

---

[6] For further discussion of the position in Northern Ireland see Frank Cranmer and Sharon Thompson, 'Marriage and Civil Partnership in Northern Ireland: A Changing Legal Landscape' [2018] *Child and Family Law Quarterly* 301.

deputy registrars of marriages. Article 31(3) also permits local authorities, at the direction of the Registrar General, to 'appoint additional persons to solemnise civil marriages and carry out other functions for the purposes of this Order'.

On its face, the Marriage (Northern Ireland) Order 2003 does not permit non-religious organisations to solemnise marriage. This was subject to a challenge by humanists in *Re Smyth's Application for Judicial Review*,[7] in which it was held that being married by a humanist celebrant was a manifestation of the applicant's religion or belief under Article 9 of the European Convention on Human Rights. However, it was held that no discrimination had actually occurred, since Article 31(3) of the Marriage (Northern Ireland) Order 2003 allowed for humanist celebrants to be appointed as the additional persons. This decision has been criticised by Sharon Thompson and Frank Cranmer as a missed opportunity for triggering reform on the basis of what 'might be described as a loophole in the 2003 Order'.[8] The use of the 'additional persons' provision opens the door to ceremonies solemnised by belief organisations, but without any restrictions as to who these additional persons can be. It remains to be seen whether and how additional persons will be appointed and whether the line will be drawn at belief systems.

Jersey

A similar approach is taken in Jersey, where there is a nomination system for religious officials while humanists are covered by the rules on civil celebrants. The difference is that in Jersey there is also a system of individual application. Like

---

7   [2018] NICA 25.
8   Sharon Thompson and Frank Cranmer, 'Humanist Weddings in Northern Ireland: A Missed Opportunity for Reform?' (2019) 41 (2) *Journal of Social Welfare and Family Law* 229, 231.

the Law Commission's proposals, the Jersey model includes independent celebrants by allowing them to individually apply to be authorised, but, unlike the Law Commission's proposal, and indeed unlike the Scottish and Irish models, the distinction is not drawn between religion and belief. Article 6 of the Marriage and Civil Status (Jersey) Law 2001 (as amended by the Marriage and Civil Status (Jersey) Order 2018) provides that marriages can be solemnised by only four groups of people: (a) the Superintendent Registrar or a Deputy Superintendent Registrar; (b) a clergyman (defined under section 1 as the Dean of Jersey, a priest or a deacon of the Anglican Church); (c) an authorised civil celebrant; or (d) an authorised religious official. Article 24A provides that a register must be kept of authorised civil celebrants and authorised religious officials, and the religious organisation that applied for the authorisation of the religious official.

Article 7 provides that a scheme for the authorisation by the Superintendent Registrar of persons as authorised civil celebrants or authorised religious officials will be prescribed. It further states that those who were authorised to solemnise marriages in registered buildings immediately before this new scheme came into force shall be deemed to be an authorised religious official for a period of 12 months. This provides a template for such a continuity provision that would be needed in the case of any reform to the law in England and Wales, though it might be asked whether there is a need to place a time limit on it. Article 3 of the Marriage and Civil Status (Jersey) Order 2018 provides that 'an individual who wishes to be authorized as an authorized civil celebrant shall apply to the Superintendent Registrar for such authorization' and outlines how this will operate. Again, this is a useful template, should reform in England and Wales include a system of individual application.

The Law Commission consultation paper is critical of the Jersey approach (and, by implication, the Northern Ireland approach), which treats humanist celebrants as civil celebrants on the basis that because they 'act as civil celebrants, rather than formally representing non-religious belief organisations' this results in 'treating non-religious belief organisations differently from religious ones' (para 5.119). Yet, under the Law Commission's schema, independent celebrants would be treated in this way and it can be argued that humanist celebrants have more in common with independent celebrants than religious ones.

Guernsey

The law in Guernsey has been reformed by The Marriage (Bailiwick of Guernsey) Law, 2020. This provides that a marriage can be solemnised by the Registrar-General, a civil celebrant, a clerk in Holy Orders of the Church of England, or an authorised religious official nominated by the relevant governing authority of any other religious organisation (Article 5). A register of civil celebrants and authorised religious officials will be kept under Article 8. This system follows Jersey in providing a further example of belief celebrants being protected as civil celebrants who are individually appointed. Article 11 is also potentially useful in that it provides for a continuity clause whereby 'a person who, immediately before the commencement of this Law, was an authorised person with reference to a licensed building' under the previous law is 'deemed to be an authorised religious official' for the purpose of the new law.

Comparative analysis of neighbouring jurisdictions shows that there is no common approach but that the current approach in England and Wales is by far the most limited. The possibility of reform should be grabbed, since the opportunity will not arise often. Indeed, unlike several other neighbouring jurisdictions, England and Wales did not use the opportunity of the introduction of civil partnerships and/or same-sex marriage laws to make such changes. Each of the jurisdictions noted here have adopted a system for marriage solemnisation that uses a combination of three types of recognition. For comparative purposes these might be termed as follows: (1) prescribed status: where law or guidance stipulates that certain persons, groups or persons within groups are entitled to solemnise marriages; (2) nominating system: where organisations need to nominate persons (or offices within their organisation) to a State body who may then bestow upon those individuals (or officeholders as a whole within the organisations) the entitlement to solemnise marriages; and (3) individual application: where individuals themselves apply to a State body for permission to solemnise marriages. Adopting these labels, the position across all of the jurisdictions noted may be compared against the Law Commission's proposals as shown in Table 7.1 This comparison underlines that there is a degree of consensus and some divergence in these approaches. All jurisdictions have moved towards a nominating system at least in part. It is noticeable that the nominating system is the means by which religious marriages are recognised in most jurisdictions (though in some, some religious groups are prescribed). Where belief marriages are recognised, they tend (with the exception of Scotland) to be part of a nominating system except in Jersey and Guernsey, where an individual application system is followed for all civil celebrants. In terms of reform of the law in England and Wales, there is a need not simply to level up to one of the various comparative options but to design a system that builds upon the strengths of the systems elsewhere and the lessons learnt in order to go further and to make such reforms that will be long lasting.

Proposed reform

The proposed reform is that, unlike in the Law Commission's proposals, officiants would be appointed in the future in one of two ways: by a nominating organisation or by individual application. The need for a separate prescribed–status category can be overcome by providing for State officials to be appointed and by the use of continuity provisions. Continuity provisions would ensure that religions that already solemnise marriages would be automatically included as nominating organisations and that individuals who already conduct marriages would be automatically included as officiants, subject to requirements for ongoing training. The Guernsey model provides an excellent model in this regard. Provision would also need to be made so that existing provisions concerning religious same-sex marriages would continue to apply.

Table 7.1: Comparison of means of appointment

	(1) Prescribed status	(2) Nominating system	(3) Individual application
Law Commission Proposals	• State officials • Anglican clergy	• All other religions and beliefs	• Independent officiants
Scotland	• State officials • Church of Scotland clergy • Prescribed religious or belief bodies	• All other religions and beliefs	
Ireland	• State officials	• All other religions • Secular bodies	
Northern Ireland	• State officials • Additional persons	• All other religions	
Jersey	• State officials • Anglican clergy	• All other religions	• Civil celebrants
Guernsey	• State officials • Anglican clergy	• All other religions	• Civil celebrants

The nominating organisation would not be limited to religion or belief organisations and would therefore also include umbrella organisations of independent celebrants and indeed any other organisation that wished to solemnise marriages. This would overcome the problems with the definitions of religion or belief and the question of whether and how independent celebrants can fit within the system. Such an approach would not place too much of a burden upon registration officials, especially if continuity provisions are included so that religions that already marry are automatically included. Limiting the types of organisation who can nominate does not make sense once the system allows independent officiants to personally apply to be able to solemnise.

Extending the law to all organisations (rather than just religion or belief organisations) is probably the most controversial element of the proposal and might be seen as opening the floodgates to a large number of new organisations with no thresholds in place. Yet, the Law Commission's proposals, which do limit nominating organisations to religion or belief organisations, also suffers from this same problem in that the inadequate definition of belief and the low threshold imposed would also open the floodgates, coupled with a truly officiant-focused approach for independent celebrants that could place a significant burden on registration officials. Extending nominating organisations beyond religion or belief organisations would be preferable to this, if safeguards are put in place.

Giving the right to solemnise marriage to nominating organisations generally would not necessarily open the floodgates. A threshold could be put in place by insisting that nominating organisations do not have the principal or sole purpose of solemnising marriages. This would follow the approach found in section 14 of the Marriage (Same Sex Couples) Act 2013, which defined 'belief organisation' as 'an organisation whose principal or sole purpose is the advancement of a system of non-religious beliefs which relate to morality or ethics', and aspects of the Irish approach, though, rather than using the term 'secular', recognition would simply be given to organisations. This would exclude organisations set up solely to solemnise marriages.[9] This would not necessarily exclude independent celebrants, provided that they carried out other services. This would address concerns about the commercialisation of weddings.

However, an argument could be advanced on human rights grounds that protection should be afforded only to religious or belief organisations. If this was followed, then it would be important to have a rigorous definition of religion or belief and a significant threshold. This needs to be counterbalanced against the risk of taking an overly conservative approach, which would indirectly discriminate against new forms of religiosity or belief. The Irish model again would be a useful template in this regard. The law could require that the organisation has the principal or sole purpose of advancing a system of religious or non-religious beliefs and that they have a set number of adherents or have existed for a set number of years.

There may still be a need for individual applications by genuinely independent celebrants, but that would be much reduced if the nominating system includes non-religious organisations and therefore most independent celebrants. In terms of the individual application system, the Jersey and Guernsey systems provide a template for how this could be achieved with an individual application process for civil celebrants if that is felt advisable.

The scheme proposed could be drafted in legislation in the following form (which adapts the legislation of neighbouring jurisdictions cited earlier).

---

[9] Though some thought would be required as to how to draw the line in relation to political organisations.

1. Registered officiants

(1) The following may be recognised as Registered Officiants:
   (a) a 'superintendent registrar', an officer appointed by a local authority;
   (b) a 'nominated official' under section 2, appointed by the Registrar General;
   (c) an 'individual applicant' under section 3, appointed by the Registrar General.
(2) A marriage between persons of different sexes may be solemnised by and only by a registered officiant.
(3) A marriage between persons of the same sex may be solemnised by and only by a registered officiant where:
   (a) the officiant is a superintendent registrar or an individual applicant;
   (b) the officiant is a nominated official and the nominating organisation has opted in for the purpose of Marriage (Same Sex Couples) Act 2013.
(4) A marriage between persons of the same sex may not be solemnised by a registered officiant who is nominated by the Church of England or the Church in Wales.

2. Nominated officials

(1) An organisation that wishes an official to be authorised as Registered Officiant shall apply to the Registrar General for registration as a recognised officiant either of a member named in the application who is aged 18 years or above or of an office within the group where it is held by a person who is aged 18 years or above.
(2) An organisation may apply to the Registrar General for a temporary authorisation to solemnise:
   (a) one or more marriages specified in the authorisation, or
   (b) marriages during a specified period so specified.
   Provided that the person of the organisation named is aged 18 years or more.

(3) Where an organisation has more than one person registered in the Register, the organisation shall not make a further application unless it is satisfied that there is a need for a larger number of its persons to be so registered.

(4) For the purposes of this Act, a body shall be a organisation if it is an organised group of people and:

(a) it has no fewer than 50 members;

(b) its principal or sole purpose is not the solemnisation of marriage;

(c) members of the body meet regularly in furtherance of the objects;

(d) it does not have rules regarding marriage or the solemnisation of marriage that contravene the requirements of this Act or any other enactment or rule of law;

(e) it is a body which, on the date of making its application, has been in existence for a continuous period of no less than five years;

(f) it has appropriate procedures in writing for selecting, training and accrediting members as fit and proper persons to solemnise marriages;

(g) it maintains a register of its members.

(5) None of the following is an organisation for the purposes of this Act:

(a) a political party, or a body that promotes a political party or candidate;

(b) a body that exists mainly to promote a political cause;

(c) a trade union or representative body of employers;

(e) a chamber of commerce;

(f) a body that promotes purposes that are:

(i) unlawful;

(ii) contrary to public morality;

(iii) in support terrorism or terrorist activities; or

(v) for the benefit of an organisation membership of which is unlawful.

3. Individual applicants

(1) An individual who wishes to be authorised as a Registered Officiant shall apply to the Registrar General for such authorisation.

(2) The Registrar General shall not authorise a person as both a nominated official and an individual applicant.

4. Applications

(1) An application to the Registrar General under sections 2 and 3 shall:
   (a) be in the form approved by the Registrar General;
   (b) include any qualifications held by the applicant that are relevant; and
   (c) be accompanied by such information or documents as the Registrar General may require.

(2) Regulations shall prescribe a scheme for the authorisation by the Registrar General of persons under sections 2 and 3 which must include:
   (a) the procedures for applying to be authorised;
   (b) the matters to be taken into account in determining whether to authorise a person provisionally or fully;
   (c) such qualifications, awarded by such persons or bodies, as the Registrar General may consider appropriate;
   (d) the conditions that shall or may be imposed on the grant or renewal of an authorisation;
   (e) the training and monitoring of officiants;
   (f) the circumstances in which an authorisation shall or may be granted, renewed, suspended or revoked; and
   (g) the review or appeal of any decision to refuse to grant or renew an authorisation, impose a condition on the grant or renewal of an authorisation or suspend or revoke an authorisation.

(3) The Registrar General may require the applicant to undertake such training as the Registrar General thinks fit.

5. Register of registered officiants

(1) The Registrar General will establish and maintain a register of recognised officiants which shall be open to inspection by members of the public at all reasonable times.

(2) An authorisation of an individual as a registered officiant shall be of unlimited duration subject to suspension of the authorisation and/or revocation of the authorisation by the Registrar general.

6. Continuity provisions

(1) Every person who immediately before the coming into force of this Act who was authorised to solemnise marriages shall be deemed to deemed to be a recognised officiant, and such deemed authorisation shall, subject to suspension or termination, be of unlimited duration.

(2) The reference to 'person' in section 6(1) also includes those who hold a particular office and those who succeed them to that office.

(3) The Registrar General may require such persons to undertake such training as the Registrar General thinks fit.

If it was decided that the term 'organisation' should be limited to religion or belief organisations, then clause 2 could be amended as follows.

2. Nominated officials

(1) A religion or belief organisation that wishes an official to be authorised as Registered Officiant shall apply to the Registrar General for registration of a recognised officiant either of a member named in the application who is aged 18 years or above or of an office within the group where it is held by a person who is aged 18 years or above.

(2) An organisation may apply to the Registrar General for a temporary authorsation to solemnise:

(a) one or more marriages specified in the authorisation, or

(b) marriages during a specified period so specified.

Provided that the person of the organisation named is aged 18 years or more.

(3) Where an organisation has more than one person registered in the Register, the organisation shall not make a further application unless it is satisfied that there is a need for a larger number of its persons to be so registered.

(4) For the purposes of this Act, a body shall be a religious organisation if it is an organised group of people and:

(a) it has not fewer than 50 members;

(b) its principal or sole purpose is the advancement of a system of spiritual beliefs which relates to morality or ethics;

(c) members of the body meet regularly in relation to their beliefs and in furtherance of the objects referred to in para (b);

(d) it does not have rules regarding marriage or the solemnisation of marriage that contravene the requirements of this Act or any other enactment or rule of law;

(e) it is a body which, on the date of making its application, has been in existence for a continuous period of not less than five years;

(f) it has appropriate procedures in writing for selecting, training and accrediting members as fit and proper persons to solemnise marriages;

(g) it maintains a register of its members.

(5) For the purposes of this Act, a body shall be a belief organisation if it is an organised group of people and:

(a) it has not fewer than 50 members;

(b) its principal or sole purpose is the advancement of a system of non-religious beliefs which relates to morality or ethics;

(c) members of the body meet regularly in relation to their beliefs and in furtherance of the objects referred to in para (b);

(d) it does not have rules regarding marriage or the solemnisation of marriage that contravene the requirements of this Act or any other enactment or rule of law;

(e) it is a body which, on the date of making its application, has been in existence for a continuous period of not less than five years;

(f) it has appropriate procedures in writing for selecting, training and accrediting members as fit and proper persons to solemnise marriages;

(g) it maintains a register of its members.

(6) None of the following is a religion or belief organisation for the purposes of this Act:

(a) a political party, or a body that promotes a political party or candidate;

(b) body that exists mainly to promote a political cause;

(c) a trade union or representative body of employers;

(e) a chamber of commerce;

(f) a body that promotes purposes that are:

(i) unlawful;

(ii) contrary to public morality;

(iii) in support terrorism or terrorist activities; or

(v) for the benefit of an organisation membership of which is unlawful.

Conclusion

This chapter has explored reform proposals in relation to the law of weddings. The Law Commission's suggestions in relation to the creation of the legal role of the officiant and the focus on rigorous preliminaries allowing a minimalistic approach to the regulation of where and how couples get married have been adopted. These changes would make a real difference in achieving the first point of principle. They would reduce the likelihood of unregistered religious marriages occurring because current restrictions would be lifted. Unregistered religious marriages that occur because of those restrictions or those that occur unwittingly because the couple are not aware of the restrictions would be reduced. That would still leave some unregistered religious marriages, however, and since some of these may not be entirely voluntary then there is a need for further safeguards, and this will be addressed in the next chapter.

It is in terms of our second point of principle that the Law Commission's proposals come up short. The paper's proposals on defining belief organisations and dealing separately with independent celebrants will not work. Once independent celebrants are afforded the right to solemnise marriage using a system of individual application, it is inconsistent to then limit nominating organisations to religions or belief organisations and to impose requirements on those organisations. This chapter has suggested that this can be overcome by allowing all organisations to nominate and that this could include the majority of independent celebrants.

Once individual applications are permitted, then there would be non-State officials conducting legally binding marriages who do not belong to a religion or belief organisation. This then makes it unsustainable to limit nominating organisations to religion or belief organisations, since representatives of other organisations can obtain officiant status by the individual application route. This is a significant flaw in the Law Commission's proposals and why opening nominations to all organisations would be preferable to limiting them to religion or belief organisations.

EIGHT

Reforming Validity and Criminal Offences

Introduction

This chapter turns to the fourth and fifth reform proposals. While the proposals discussed in the last chapter were directly concerned with how people get married, the proposals discussed here are concerned with related laws which concern the effect and regulation of marriage: looking at the law on what constitutes a valid marriage and possible criminal offences. The proposals discussed in the previous chapter will not be sufficient to overcome the problem of unregistered religious marriages which are entered into unwittingly or involuntarily. The proposals discussed here and in the next chapter serve as backstops to provide further protection in such a scenario.

The two backstops discussed here, the law on validity and criminal offences, would be needed less if the sixth proposal is enacted and there is reform of cohabitation rights. For that reason, cohabitation law reform is discussed separately in the next chapter. Of the two backstops discussed in this chapter, the law on validity is the most crucial. However, new criminal offences have been seen as the answer to the problem of unregistered marriages, most notably by the Independent Review and a number of commentators, as well as in the provisions of Baroness Cox's Marriage Act 1949 (Amendment) Bill. Yet, criminal offences will have a very limited effect, limited to just preventing and discouraging certain forms of behaviour. The most appropriate remedy is not criminal at all but is about providing appropriate rights on relationship breakdown. The reforms presented in this part are designed as a package: implementing just the criminal law provisions would have very little effect.

The law on validity

Provisions on validity can mitigate the problem of unregistered religious marriage by declaring such marriages either valid or void (rather than non-qualifying ceremonies) and there-fore enabling the parties to seek legal redress on relationship breakdown. The current law on validity is complex and the Court of Appeal in *Attorney General v Akhter*[1] took the view that any formulation of what actions would cumulatively lead to a marriage being void rather than non-qualifying would be unwise, since the Court 'would not want to encourage parties who want to marry to rely on such partially compliant ceremonies because the outcome will, inevitably, be uncertain' (para 66). Yet, a lack of clarity as to the difference between void and non-qualifying ceremonies will actually frustrate legal certainty. The Court of Appeal also stated that: 'Certainty as to the existence of a marriage is in the interests of the parties to a ceremony and of the State. Indeed, it could be said that [this is] the main purpose of the regulatory framework' (para 10). Given the developing case law on 'non-marriage'[2] (which

---

[1]   [2020] EWCA Civ 122.
[2]   See further Rebecca Probert, 'The Evolving Concept of Non-Marriage' [2013] *Child and Family Law Quarterly* 314.

the Court of Appeal relabelled 'non-qualifying ceremonies'), there is a need to be able to elucidate what the legal position is.

The Law Commission's call to codify and simplify the law on validity should therefore be followed. The law as it currently stands is inconsistent and unprincipled. Rules on validity need to apply across all purported marriages. Yet, there is a need to go further than the Law Commission's proposals. As discussed in Part II, the Law Commission's proposed codification of the law on validity can be recast as saying that the status of an opposite-sex marriage depends on the answers to three questions.

(1) Have both parties given notice?
(2) Do both or one of the parties believe that the officiant is authorised?
(3) Have both parties given consent?

Under the Law Commission's schema, the absence of (1) or (2) will render the marriage void; the absence of (3) will make a marriage voidable or non-qualifying, while the absence of (1) and (2) or the absence of all three requirements will render the ceremony non-qualifying. These rules could be clarified further. In particular, contrary to the Law Commission's proposals, it should not be a valid marriage where only one of the parties believes that there is an authorised officiant at the wedding. The Law Commission suggests that such a marriage should be valid in order to protect the duped spouse. However, sufficient protection would be given if such a marriage was declared void. This could mean that the law on the status of an opposite-sex marriage depends on the answers to three questions.

(1) Have both parties given notice?
(2) Did both parties believe that the officiant is authorised?
(3) Have both parties given consent?

The absence of (1) or (2) will render the marriage void; the absence of (3) will make a marriage voidable or non-qualifying; the absence of (1) and (2) or the absence of all three requirements will render the ceremony non-qualifying. This could be presented in legislation as follows.

1. Validity

(1) A valid marriage will exist where both of the parties:
   (a) give notice before the wedding;
   (b) believe that there is an authorised officiant at the wedding; and
   (c) express consent at the wedding.
(2) A void marriage will exist where either 1(a) or (b) has not been met but the other two requirements have been met.
(3) A non-qualifying marriage will exist where 1(c) is not met and/or where both 1(a) and (b) have not been met.
(4) A marriage will be voidable where the consent is vitiated by duress, mistake, impaired mental capacity or similar other factors.

These provisions would go some way to fulfilling our principle that unregistered religious marriages are of concern where there has not been a free and informed choice to opt out of legal protection. Couples misled by the presumed officiant would have a valid marriage under this approach, and where one party has misled the other in this regard then the marriage would be void rather than non-qualifying. However, under this proposal there will still be unregistered religious marriages that are non-qualifying. These proposals would have made no direct difference to the outcome of *Akhter v Khan*, for instance. This points to the limited effect that changes to the law on validity can have (unless an overly generous approach is taken that effectively makes all purported marriages legally binding – and this would cause issues in terms of legal certainty as well as for those couples who enter into religious marriages with the intention that their union will not be legally binding). The law on validity can and should be stretched only so far. A preferable and more effective approach of providing further relief would be to reform the law on cohabitation. This is not to deny, however, that some stretching of the law on validity and codifying it in a way that leads to certainty would be advantageous. It is a useful backstop, but a limited one.

Criminal offences

Contrary to calls for reform often made that see the enactment of criminal provisions as the solution to the problem of unregistered religious marriages, the criminal law actually provides an even more limited backstop than the law on validity. Criminal law by its nature penalises and punishes behaviour. It does not provide the remedies that are necessary in the case of an unregistered religious marriage: punishing wedding officials or even parties to a marriage does not provide remedies to the disadvantaged purported spouse on relationship breakdown. Caution should be taken in recommending the enactment of new criminal offences, since there is a risk that such provisions will be focused upon and erroneously seen as 'the answer'. Moreover, it is often the case that many proposed new criminal offences would penalise behaviour that is already a criminal offence.[3]

This means that, rather than suggesting that a new criminal offence is created, it would be preferable to amend existing criminal offences to make it clear that they apply to the situations that need to be criminalised. There are three such amendments that need to be made. It could be argued that at least some of these are, at most, clarifications, in that the situation is already probably covered by the existing offence.

---

[3] Indeed, there are already a number of offences found in the Marriage Act 1949. These may need some amendment as a result of other changes to weddings law such as a move to an officiant system.

The need for an amendment could therefore be questioned. However, for clarity, it would be preferable that this was explicitly laid out, whether in a new statute such as the mooted Intimate Adult Relationships Act or by amending the original criminal provisions. The three amendments are as follows.

Forced marriages

Under section 121(1) of the Antisocial Behaviour, Crime and Policing Act 2014, it is an offence in England and Wales for a defendant to use violence, threats or any other form of coercion for the purpose of causing another person to enter into a marriage where the defendant believes, or ought reasonably to believe, that the conduct may cause the other person to enter into the marriage without free and full consent. The defendant's actions need not be directed at the victim (s121(6)). Under section 121(2), where the victim lacks capacity to consent (as defined under the Mental Capacity Act 2005) the offence is 'capable of being committed by any conduct carried out for the purpose of causing the victim to enter into a marriage (whether or not the conduct amounts to violence, threats or any other form coercion)'. Under section 121(3), it is an offence where the defendant practises any form of deception with the intention of causing another person to leave the United Kingdom, and intends the other person to be subjected to conduct outside the United Kingdom that would be an offence under section 121(1) or would have been so had the victim been in England and Wales.

Section 121(4) states that '"marriage" means any religious or civil ceremony of marriage (whether or not legally binding)', providing rare statutory recognition of marriages that are not legally binding. The Law Commission consultation paper noted that this means that 'forcing someone into a religious-only marriage is potentially a criminal offence'.[4] However,

---

[4] Law Commission, *Getting Married: A Consultation Paper on Weddings Law* (Consultation Paper 247, 2020) para 10.199.

they noted that there would be 'no implications for the status of the marriage' and that the existence of the provision therefore does not 'provide much assistance in deciding when a religious-only ceremony should be recognised for the purpose of financial provision'. This is true. Providing a remedy on relationship breakdown is not the purpose of the offence. However, this does not mean that the offence cannot be useful in terms of discouraging and prohibiting the use of violence, threats or any other coercion to cause another person to enter into a marriage.[5] The offence as drafted clearly criminalises the situation where one party is forced into a civil or religious marriage ceremony. It would not, however, seem to cover the situation where someone is forced not to have a civil wedding ceremony. This could be usefully clarified.

Coercive control

Under section 76(1) of the Serious Crime Act 2015, it is an offence for a person (A) to repeatedly or continuously engage in behaviour towards another person (B) that is controlling or coercive, where at the time of the behaviour A and B are personally connected, the behaviour has a serious effect on B, and A knows or ought to know that the behaviour will have a serious effect on B. Section 76(2) states that A and B are personally connected if they are in 'an intimate personal relationship' or if they live together and are members of the same family or have previously been in an intimate personal relationship with each other. Under section 76(4), behaviour is deemed to have a 'serious effect' on B if it causes B to fear, on at least two occasions, that violence will be used against B, or it causes B serious alarm or distress which has

---

[5]   Forced Marriage Protection Orders are also of use, on which see Family Law Act 1996 Part 4 (as inserted by the Forced Marriage (Civil Protection) Act 2007).

a substantial adverse effect on B's usual day-to-day activities. It is a defence under section 76(8) if it can be shown that in engaging in the behaviour in question, A believed that he or she was acting in B's best interests and the behaviour was in all the circumstances reasonable. This does not apply in relation to behaviour that causes B to fear that violence will be used against B. This defence will apply if the contrary is not proved beyond reasonable doubt.

Section 76(6) states that A and B are members of the same family if they are, or have been, married to each other; they are, or have been, civil partners of each other; they are relatives; they have agreed to marry one another; they have entered into a civil partnership agreement; they are both parents of the same child; or they have, or have had, parental responsibility for the same child. The provision in section 121(4) of the Antisocial Behaviour, Crime and Policing Act 2014, which makes it clear that marriage for this purpose includes any marriage ceremony, whether or not it is legally binding, could be helpfully duplicated here.

This offence can complement the law on forced marriage by articulating what constitutes coercive behaviour in intimate adult relationships. It can also be of use in terms of discouraging such behaviour. This offence has already been raised in the context of religious marriages. In January 2020 it was reported that a Jewish wife had launched a private prosecution under section 76 of the Serious Crime Act 2015 against her ex-husband who denied her a religious divorce.[6] The judge accepted an application for the State to fund prosecution costs, but the case was discontinued after the ex-husband gave the religious divorce. The fact that the prosecution did not go ahead means that it is unknown whether this action or one like it would

---

[6] See https://www.thejc.com/news/uk-news/landmark-case-sees-woman-obtain-get-after-launching-private-prosecution-against-husband-for-coercive-1.495362

be successful (and whether it would apply to religious-only marriages). However, the wife's solicitor, Gary Lesin-Davis, is quoted as saying that the offence 'can provide a powerful remedy to protected vulnerable women whose treatment by recalcitrant husbands strays into criminal offending'.

Fraud

The offences discussed so far would criminalise the situation where the defendant forces or coerces the claimant to enter into a non-qualifying marriage. Yet, in the debate on the problem of unregistered religious marriages, more attention has been afforded to the perceived need to criminalise the actions of the celebrant (or officiant under the Law Commission's schema). For some, there is a need to criminalise all religious marriages that take place without or before a marriage following the requirements of the Marriage Act 1949 has taken place. However, not only would this criminalise unregistered religious marriages that take place voluntarily but it would also criminalise other marriage ceremonies that currently take place that are not under the Marriage Act 1949, such as those by humanist and independent celebrants.

The Law Commission's paper is particularly useful in articulating the gap where an offence might be needed. Such an offence, however, is already covered by the provisions of the Fraud Act 2006. Section 2 provides for the offence of fraud by false representation. This applies where the defendant dishonestly makes a false representation and intends, by making the representation, to make a gain for himself or another, or to cause loss to another or to expose another to a risk of loss. This could cover the situation where the defendant either is an officiant or purports to be an officiant and dishonestly makes a false representation as to the status or the effect of the ceremony intending to make a gain for himself or another, or to cause loss to another or to expose another to a risk of loss. It might be useful to clarify in any legislation seeking to deal with unregistered religious marriage that this scenario would be covered by the law on fraud. Such an approach would also reduce the risk that recommendations relating to new criminal offences are seen as the main or only solution to the issue.

Conclusion

The need for codification of the law to achieve modernisation and consistency applies as much to the law on validity and criminal offences concerned with marriages as it does to the law on getting married. Changes to both the law on validity and criminal offences are suggested by the Law Commission but these suggestions will not be sufficient. The law on validity requires further simplification, while in relation to criminal offences the focus needs to be on amending and applying existing offences rather than creating new ones which run the risk of being seen as 'the solution'. The reforms suggested in this chapter are backstops, providing some protection for unregistered religious marriages that remain outside the schema presented in the previous chapter. The difference that they will make is limited, but they would provide some further protection to unregistered religious marriages that are not wittingly or voluntarily entered into. However, greater protection would be afforded by cohabitation reform, as the next chapter will discuss.

NINE

Reforming Cohabitation Rights

Introduction

This chapter turns to the sixth reform proposal and this is in many ways the most important one. The introduction of the kind of cohabitation rights found in neighbouring jurisdictions would do much to alleviate the problem of unregistered religious marriages. Modernisation of wedding law should reduce the number of unwitting unregistered religious marriages or such marriages that occur because existing legal formalities provide a hurdle. By contrast, cohabitation rights on relationship breakdown would provide a remedy to those who are in unregistered religious marriages where the decision not to enter into a legal marriage has not been entered into voluntarily or where the relationship has changed over time so that one party has become reliant on the other or has suffered a detriment as a result of the relationship. This would apply, for instance, where one party has given up paid work, reduced their hours or forgone promotion in order to raise children, keep the home and/or to look after the other party. These detriments are likely to be gendered and can often be subtle.

However, it is also important not to take a too paternalistic approach. It is vital that cohabitation rights do not trample upon the free choice of the parties. If the parties have made an autonomous choice not to marry and be subject to the rules and obligations that come with marital status, then this should be respected. The lead of other jurisdictions should be followed to allow couples to opt out of such cohabitation-based protection while also ensuring that this is voluntary and fair. This opt-out rather than opt-in requirement would ensure that cohabitation rights are afforded to couples who are choosing to cohabit thinking that they would be entitled to 'common law marriage' rights, as well as those where there is an intention to marry but the couple do not get around to it. The safeguard that the opt-out agreement must be voluntary and fair would also allow changing circumstances and power dynamics to be taken into account.

Although the reforms discussed in previous chapters would have the effect of reducing the number of unregistered religious marriages, some would still exist and those couples would be in the same position as cohabitants. Reforming the law relating to cohabitation is needed not only in the context of unregistered religious marriages but more generally. Like unregistered religious marriages, people enter into cohabiting relationships for a variety of reasons and have different views as to whether they will also seek a legally recognised marriage. And, like unregistered religious marriages, cohabitation generally can often lead to detriment and, if it has not been wittingly and voluntarily entered into then the law should respond to this. This chapter will explain what sort of reform is needed and will pay attention to different approaches that exist or have been suggested.

Cohabitation rights

As Joanna Miles has noted, 'cohabiting couples in English law exist in a sort of halfway house: recognized for some legal purposes, but not others'.[1] In some respects, cohabiting couples

---

[1] Joanna Miles, ' "Cohabitants" in the Law of England and Wales: A Brief Introduction', in Rajnaara C. Akhtar, Patrick Nash and Rebecca

already enjoy significant legal rights: many Acts of Parliament (such as section 1(1A) of the Inheritance (Provision for Family and Dependents Act) 1975) bestow rights on couples who live together 'as if' they were husband and wife; laws relating to children and criminal offences within the family largely make no distinction between couples who are married and those who are not; and cohabitants receive 'quite extensive legal recognition where one partner dies, though this is less generous than for widowed spouses'.[2] As Miles points out, 'the difference in the treatment of cohabitants and spouses is most stark and well known on relationship breakdown'. Other than where there are children as a result of the relationship or where the couple have been renting, if a cohabiting relationship breaks down then any financial and property disputes are dealt with through the law of property. This means that 'the simple question is "who owns what?" and the court is only concerned to answer that question, not to consider who *should* get what, applying any sort of "fairness" consideration of the sort that applies on divorce'.[3] Unlike married couples, cohabiting couples – including those who are have entered into unregistered religious marriages[4] – who split up must often navigate complex trust law principles that depend on direct financial contribution.

The call for cohabitation rights, therefore, more specifically focuses on what the Law Commission termed 'a statutory scheme for the adjustment of property rights or financial provision between cohabiting couples on separation'.[5] Such

---

Probert (eds), *Cohabitation and Religious Marriage* (Bristol University Press, 2020) 27, 37.

[2] Ibid 33.

[3] Ibid 35.

[4] This is shown in *Amin v Amin* [2020] EWHC 2675 (Ch), which concerned a nikah religious marriage.

[5] Law Commission, *Cohabitation: The Financial Consequences of Relationship Breakdown* (Law Com No 307, 2007) para 1.5.

reform has been long mooted and supported by family law practitioners and academics. For instance, in a landmark book Anne Barlow, Simon Duncan, Grace James and Alison Park argued that relationship-generated disadvantage can occur in both married and unmarried relationships, and so cohabitation rights on separation are needed to protect the economically disadvantaged partner.[6]

Different approaches

The most detailed discussion of how rights for cohabiting couples could be realised can be found by looking at the schemes that apply in other jurisdictions and the model proposed by the Law Commission. The following will outline the systems that apply in Scotland and Ireland before looking at the Law Commission's proposed reform and two recent private Member's bills. The differences between the approaches discussed are not vast and so, taken as a whole, these examples show clearly how such rights could be introduced into English law.

The Scottish model

The Family Law (Scotland) Act 2006 provides that a former cohabitant can apply for compensation if she or he has suffered economic disadvantage, and his or her partner has experienced economic advantage, both directly as a result of the cohabitation. Section 25 defines a cohabitant as either member of a couple who are or were 'living together as if they were husband and wife' or as if they were civil partners. It states that, in determining this, the court shall have regard to the period

---

[6]   Anne Barlow, Simon Duncan, Grace James and Alison Park, *Cohabitation, Marriage and the Law: Social Change and Legal Reform in the 21st Century* (Hart, 2005).

in which they have lived together, the nature of their relationship during that period and the nature and extent of any
financial arrangements subsisting, or which subsisted, during
that period. There would be a rebuttable presumption that
each cohabitant has a right to an equal share in household
goods acquired other than by gift or succession from a third
party, excluding money, securities, vehicles or domestic animals
(section 26). In relation to money and property (other than
their sole or main residence) this is to be treated as belonging
to each cohabitant in equal shares, subject to any agreement
between the cohabitants to the contrary (section 27).

If the cohabitation ends for any reason other than death,
then a cohabitant can apply to the court for a financial order
requiring the defender to pay a financial award for a specific
amount (section 28). In determining whether to grant an order
the court will take into account 'whether (and, if so, to what
extent) the defender has derived economic advantage from
contributions made by the applicant; and whether (and, if so,
to what extent) the applicant has suffered economic disadvantage in the interests of the defender; or any relevant child'.
Economic advantage includes gains in capital, income and
earning capacity. The application needs to take place no later
than one year after the day on which the cohabitants cease to
cohabit. There is no right to opt out in the Act itself but it is
thought that it is possible under the general law for cohabitants to opt out of these provisions by making an agreement.[7]

There has been some controversy about how the system has
operated in practice. A discussion paper by the Scottish Law
Commission in February 2020 surveyed a number of changes
including introducing a qualifying period for cohabitation, a
list of features to be taken into account in determining whether

---

[7] Fran Wasoff, Jo Miles and Enid Mordaunt, *Legal Practitioners' Perspectives on
the Cohabitation Provisions of the Family Law (Scotland) Act 2006* (Nuffield
Foundation, 2010) 142.

a couple are cohabitants and extending the time limit.[8] This later point has also been raised by the Law Society of Scotland, who suggested that section 28 be amended to allow a court to accept an application made after the one-year time limit 'on cause shown'.[9]

However, it has also been pointed out that England and Wales has much to learn from the existing Scottish model. As Lady Hale noted in *Gow v Grant*,[10] the remedy provided is 'both practicable and fair' and 'does not impose upon unmarried couples the responsibilities of marriage but redresses the gains and losses flowing from their relationship' (para 56). It has 'undoubtedly achieved a lot for Scottish cohabitants and their children'. In *Gow v Grant* Lord Hope stressed that the intention had been to provide a 'limited' right because there 'was a respectable body of opinion that it would be unwise to impose marriage-like legal consequences on couples who had deliberately chosen not to marry' (para 4). He held that although section 28 'lacks any reference to fairness as the guiding principle', its 'background shows that this is what was intended by the legislature' (para 31). The underlying rationale is that 'it would be unfair to let economic gains and losses arising out of contributions or sacrifices made in the course of a relationship simply lie where they fell'.

The Irish model

The Civil Partnership and Certain Rights and Obligations of Cohabitants Act 2010 provides similar protection for cohabitants, defined under section 172 as two adults 'who live together

---

[8] Scottish Law Commission, *Aspects of Family Law: Discussion Paper on Cohabitation* (February 2020).
[9] Law Society of Scotland, *Rights of Cohabitants: Family Law (Scotland) Act 2006, Sections 28 and 29* (March 2019).
[10] [2012] UKSC 29.

as a couple in an intimate and committed relationship and who are not related to each other within the prohibited degrees of relationship or married to each other or civil partners of each other'. In determining whether or not two adults are cohabitants, 'the court shall take into account all the circumstances of the relationship' but should have particular regard to the duration of the relationship, the basis on which they live together, the degree of financial dependence, the degree and nature of any financial arrangements between them, whether there are dependent children, whether one adult cares for and supports the children of the other and 'the degree to which the adults present themselves to others as a couple'. They must have lived with each other for two years or more if they had dependent children or five years or more if not. This is a more detailed list than in the Scottish model.

Section 173 provides that, subject to any cohabitation agreement that exists between them, a cohabitant can apply to the court on relationship breakdown for a financial order. This can be a property adjustment order under section 174, a compensatory maintenance order under section 175 (which could include periodic payments) or a pension readjustment order under section 187. Under section 173, an order can be granted only if the applicant satisfies the court that they are 'financially dependent on the other cohabitant and that the financial dependence arises from the relationship or the ending of the relationship, the court may, if satisfied that it is just and equitable to do so in all the circumstances, make the order concerned'. In reaching that decision, the court will have regard to 'the financial circumstances, needs and obligations of each qualified cohabitant existing as at the date of the application or which are likely to arise in the future', the rights and entitlements of any spouse, civil partner or child from a previous relationship, 'the duration of the parties' relationship, the basis on which the parties entered into the relationship and the degree of commitment of the parties to one another', contributions made, 'the effect on the earning capacity of each of the cohabitants of the responsibilities assumed by each of them during the period they lived together as a couple', any physical or mental disability of the cohabitant seeking the order and 'the conduct of each of the cohabitants, if the conduct is such that, in the opinion of the court, it would be unjust to disregard it'. This, again, is a more expansive and prescriptive list than in the Scottish model.

Law Commission proposals

The title of the Law Commission's report, *Cohabitation: The Financial Consequences of Relationship Breakdown*, shows that their proposals also share a similar focus to the Scottish and Irish models.[11] As the report noted, 'our priority should be to address the position of those who are vulnerable under the current law, and who either do not know that they must opt in to obtain protection or who are unable, for whatever reason, to do so' (para 2.86). Like the other models, the Law Commission's scheme 'would not equate cohabitants with married couples or give them equivalent rights. Nor would it provide a new status which cohabitants should sign up to in order to gain new rights' (para 1.2). As the Law Commission argued: 'If we want to remove more couples from the scope of property and trust law and the unsatisfactory outcomes that it often produces on separation, and thereby provide better basic justice between cohabitants, then an opt-in approach is not the answer' (para 2.86). The scheme is again dependent upon parties meeting a definition of cohabitant. The Law Commission proposed that this should apply 'where they are living as a couple in a joint household and (2) they are neither married to each other nor civil partners' (para 3.13). However, they rejected the notion of a statutory list of criteria to assist

---

[11] Law Commission, *Cohabitation: The Financial Consequences of Relationship Breakdown* (Law Com No 307, 2007).

with this definition, on the basis that this could 'encourage a "box-ticking mentality"', could 'lead to an undesirable degree of rigidity or confusion about the status and importance of items on the list' and was deemed unnecessary because the joint household concept can be 'readily be understood as a matter of plain English' (para3.17). They nevertheless highlighted 'some of the central factors that we think a court would wish to have in mind when deciding whether the parties' relationship was that of a couple' as being the existence of a joint household, the stability of the relationship, financial arrangements, responsibility for children, whether there is a sexual relationship and the public recognition of the relationship (paras 3.18–3.19). This, therefore, is just a different way of arriving at the same place.

The Law Commission proposed that, in addition, in order to apply for financial relief on separation cohabitants either had to have had a child together or had lived as a couple in a joint household for a duration that would be specified by statute within a range of two to five years (paras 3.31 and 3.63). They noted that 'no jurisdiction which has legislated in this field has confined remedies to cohabitants with children' and that there was 'evidence that cohabitants without children have the same potential to encounter unfairness on separation as cohabitants with children' (paras 2.81 and 2.77). Under the Law Commission's proposals, financial relief would only be granted to the cohabitant 'based upon the economic impact of cohabitation' (para 4.32). It would need to be proved that 'the respondent has a retained benefit; or the applicant has an economic disadvantage as a result of qualifying contributions the applicant has made' (para 4.33). A 'retained benefit may take the form of capital, income or earning capacity that has been acquired, retained or enhanced'; 'economic disadvantage is a present or future loss'; and 'qualifying contribution is any contribution arising from the cohabiting relationship which is made to the parties' shared lives or to the welfare of members of their families' (paras 4.35, 4.36 and 4.34).

The court would have regard to 'discretionary factors': namely the welfare of any children of both parties, which will be 'the court's first consideration'; the financial needs and obligations of both parties; the extent and nature of their financial resources; the 'welfare of any children who live with, or might reasonably be expected to live with, either party'; and the 'conduct of each party, defined restrictively' (para 4.38). The Law Commission further suggested that, in making an order, 'the court shall not place the applicant, for the foreseeable future, in a stronger economic position than the respondent' (para 4.39). Financial orders could include lump sums, property transfers and settlements, orders for sale and pension sharing but, 'unlike on divorce, periodical payments should not generally be available' (para 4.40). Where the scheme is engaged 'it should apply between the parties to the exclusion of the general law of implied trusts, estoppel and contract' (para 4.41).

The Law Commission's schema would explicitly provide for opt-out agreements. These would need to be in writing, be signed and make clear the parties' intention to disapply the statute, with pro-formas being made available (paras 5.56 and 5.58). The Law Commission noted that 'a Nikah contract written and signed by the parties, which contemplated and provided for the eventuality of separation (in particular by providing for the Mahr to be paid on divorce), would go some way to satisfying the requirements for an opt-out agreement' but would constitute an opt-out agreement only if it indicated an intention to disapply the statute (para 5.67). Agreements that purported to disapply the statute but which did 'not comply with these qualifying criteria should be of no effect when the statutory scheme is invoked' (para 5.57) and the court would also be 'entitled to set aside an opt-out agreement if its enforcement would cause manifest unfairness having regard to (1) the circumstances at the time the agreement was made; or (2) circumstances at the time the agreement comes to be enforced which were unforeseen when the agreement was made' (para 5.61). This would mean that 'it would be open to either party to claim that to enforce the contract would cause manifest unfairness having regard to the circumstances at the time the agreement was made, or at the time the agreement was being enforced' (para 5.68). Where such an opt-out agreement applies, then the parties' own financial arrangements (if any) would apply (para 2.94).

As Lady Hale noted in *Gow v Grant*,[12] 'there is some reason to think that a family law remedy such as that proposed by the Law Commission would be less costly and more productive of settlements as well as achieving fairer results than the present law' (para 47). She noted, however, that a lesson from Scotland was that 'the lack of any definition of cohabitation, or a qualifying period of cohabitation for couples who do not have children, has not proved a problem' (para 52). Moreover, for Lady Hale, the Scottish model was to be preferred over the Law Commission's proposals because their 'compensation principle, although attractive in theory, can be difficult to apply in practice because of the problems of identifying and valuing those advantages and disadvantages' (para 53). She noted that 'the flexibility inherent in the Scottish provisions is preferable to the Law Commission's proposal that the losses should be shared between them', but that, on the other hand, 'the Law Commission's proposed list of factors to be taken into account in the exercise of the court's discretion might be a useful addition to the Scottish law, as also might the power to make a periodical payments order in those rare cases where it is not practicable to make an order that a capital sum be paid by instalments' (para 55).

Private Member's bills

The Law Commission's proposals have not been taken forward. The matter has instead been the subject of two private

---

[12] [2012] UKSC 29.

Member's bills: Lord Lester's Cohabitation Bill in 2009 and Lord Marks' Cohabitation Rights Bill, which was first introduced in 2013 and mostly recently reintroduced in February 2020. Both Bills take a similar approach to that of the Scottish and Irish legislation and of the Law Commission. Both Bills define cohabitants as two people who live together as a couple and either have a child together or have lived together as a couple for a continuous period of three years or more (clause 2). They cannot be married or in civil partnerships with each other or within the degrees of relationship in relation to each other.

In relation to rights on separation, unless there is an opt-out agreement in force or deed of trust (clause 6), a former cohabitant may apply to the court for a financial settlement order within 24 months of when they ceased living together unless they satisfy the court that exceptional circumstances would justify a late application being made (clause 7). The provision on how the court may make a financial settlement order differs slightly between the two Bills. Under Lord Lester's Cohabitation Bill, an order can be made if 'having regard to all the circumstances, the court considers that it is just and equitable to make an order' (clause 8). As Lady Hale noted in *Gow v Grant*,[13] this 'would have given the courts a much wider discretion to do what was "just and equitable" having regard to all the circumstances'. By contrast, Lord Marks' Cohabitation Rights Bill follows the Law Commission's proposals, stating that an order can be made if the court is satisfied either 'that the respondent has retained a benefit, or that the applicant has an economic disadvantage, as a result of qualifying contributions the applicant has made' and 'the court considers that it is just and equitable to make an order' (clause 8). Lord Lester's Cohabitation Bill also states that 'there is to be no presumption that the applicant and the respondent

---

[13] [2012] UKSC 29 at para 53.

should share equally in property belonging to either or both of them' and that any order should reflect the principle that 'the applicant and the respondent should be self-supporting as soon as reasonably practicable, and any award made in favour of an applicant should not exceed the applicant's reasonable needs'. Both Bills say that regard is to be had to the list of discretionary factors specified in clause 9. These also differ slightly but are similar to the lists given in the Irish legislation and by the Law Commission.

Both Bills provide in clause 12 for opt-out agreements which must: contain a statement by each of the parties that they have each separately received legal advice from a qualified practitioner as to the effect of the opt-out agreement and understand its effect; agree that a financial settlement order should not be available if they cease living together as a couple and specify whether this is to apply either in all circumstances, or only to such extent, or in such circumstances, as may be specified in the agreement. The opt-out agreement must be in writing, signed and dated by both, and the signatures must be witnessed by at least one person and the agreement must be accompanied by a certificate by a qualified practitioner that the practitioner has given legal advice. An opt-out agreement which is made in the prescribed form is to be taken to comply with these requirements. Clause 13 provides that the parties can vary or revoke the opt-out agreements and clause 14 states that the court can do the same, but 'only if the court determines that the agreement is manifestly unfair to the applicant because of the circumstances in which the agreement was entered into or varied, or any change in the circumstances of either party which was unforeseen at the time the agreement was entered into or varied'.

The various approaches to cohabitation rights described earlier have much in common. They provide a statutory scheme which will apply to cohabitants on separation provided that there is no opt-out. Some systems provide more details as to the definition of the term cohabitants than others, but this tends to amount to having a child together or living together for a certain amount of time. In terms of rights on separation, the schemes allow a cohabitant to seek a financial order in certain circumstances. The broadest approach here is that found in Lord Lester's Cohabitation Bill, which simply says that an order can be made if, 'having regard to all the circumstances, the court considers that it is just and equitable to make an order'. Most approaches, however, require evidence of an advantage or disadvantage. A range of slightly different factors are then given for the court to take into account in determining this, and most approaches provide for an opt-out either implicitly or explicitly. From the synthesis of these approaches, it would be straightforward to develop a scheme of cohabitation rights on relationship breakdown in England and Wales. Indeed, the private Member's bill provisions could easily be incorporated into an Intimate Adult Relationships Act in the same way that the Scottish and Irish models are found within more general statutes.

Conclusion

Cohabitation rights upon separation with an opt-out system with safeguards would undoubtedly deal with the issues that arise from unregistered religious marriages. It would provide redress for couples who erroneously think that they are legally married or have the rights of married couples (which include those cohabitants who think they are protected by 'common law' marriage). It would also protect those who intend to marry but never do (the *Akhter v Khan* situation), as well as those who wish to marry but are frustrated by the indirectly discriminatory requirements found in the current law (though, as argued earlier, those requirements requiring marriage in a place of religious worship should be replaced). It would also ensure that those who consciously and freely decide that they do not want a legally binding marriage are not burdened with rights and responsibilities that they do not want – and the fact that it is an opt-out system with sufficient safeguards means that the freedom of that choice can be assessed.

Crucially, all of the approaches discussed allow for the relationship between cohabitants to be assessed over time. This is vital, since the relationship and the degree of reliance are likely to change over time. Any opt-out agreement would also need to be looked at in the same way. This is a concern that Sharon Thompson has raised in relation to prenuptial agreements.[14] She has put forward a new approach, which she terms Feminist Relational Contract Theory,[15] which explicitly factors in how the relationship has changed over time with particular focus on the gendered dimensions. This approach has influenced the highest court in Australia[16] and could have wider application to intimate adult relationships generally. England and Wales is behind several other jurisdictions in providing some legal redress to cohabitants on relationship breakdown. The approaches described here show how such rights could be drafted and enacted. This would do much to protect those not only in unregistered religious marriages but in cohabiting relationships generally. While reform of marriage law is needed to provide recognition of a number of relationships currently denied legal status, cohabitation rights on separation would provide a remedy for those whose relationships remain unrecognised. Both of these reforms are necessary.

---

[14] Sharon Thompson, *Prenuptial Agreements and the Presumption of Free Choice: Issues of Power in Theory and Practice* (Hart, 2015).

[15] See ibid and Sharon Thompson, 'Feminist Relational Contract Theory: A New Model for Family Property Agreements' (2018) 45 (4) *Journal of Law and Society* 617.

[16] *Thorne v Kennedy* [2017] HCA 49; see Sharon Thompson, '*Thorne v Kennedy*: Why Australia's Decision on Prenups is Important for English Law' (2018) 48 *Family Law* 415.

TEN

Conclusions: Relationship Solutions

It is difficult to dispute that the law on marriage in England and Wales is antiquated and is in need of reform. One compelling reason for reform is the fact that many wedding ceremonies now take place outside the Marriage Act 1949. Such couples then have to undergo the cost and inconvenience of undergoing an additional civil ceremony which is of little meaning to them or, even worse, they wrongly assume that the original wedding ceremony was legally binding and find out only when the relationship ends that they are denied the legal protections given to married couples. The inadequacy of the current law is underlined by two issues that have come to the fore in recent years that highlight the injustice caused by the current law: the issues of unregistered religious marriages and of non-religious marriages.

Reform is needed to deal with these issues. In relation to non-religious marriages, there is a need to give marriages conducted by belief organisations and independent celebrants legal effect. However, if ceremonies by independent celebrants are made legally binding, then there is no reason to restrict the organisations who can conduct weddings to religious or belief organisations. Permitting all organisations to nominate celebrants – including umbrella organisations representing independent celebrants – would provide the preferable way forward. However, failing that, if the law is to be limited to religion or belief organisations then a rigorous definition needs to be employed of religion or belief and recognition also needs to be given to independent celebrants. To include ceremonies by celebrants from belief organisations but to exclude ceremonies by independent celebrants would only replace one discrimination and injustice with another.

In relation to unregistered religious marriages, a step forward would be provided by removing the obstacles which currently indirectly discriminate against some religious groups which insist that such marriages must take place in a place of religious worship and use prescribed words in order to be legally binding. This would be likely to reduce the numbers of unregistered religious marriages. It would prevent those unregistered religious marriages that occur due to the strictness of the law: where the requirement for a building means that couples opt for a religious only marriage or where they are unaware of the legal requirements. However, some unregistered marriages would still exist. Some such marriages would not be problematic. Where they result from a free and deliberate choice, then the decision not to comply with legal formalities should be respected. Banning such marriages, requiring that they always follow a legal ceremony or penalising those who conduct such ceremonies would therefore be inappropriate and counterproductive, forcing such unions further into the shadows.

However, this does not mean that there is no role for English law. Legal redress should be provided to those in unregistered religious marriages where the failure to comply with registration requirements is unwitting or is not truly voluntary on the part of one of the parties. Education and awareness raising has an important part to play here but this would be aided considerably if the legal framework were accessible and principled. And, ultimately, there is a role for law here in terms of providing backstops whereby some redress can be given to those who unwittingly or involuntarily enter into unregistered religious marriages. Reform of the law of validity to make some unregistered religious marriages void could provide such a backstop and there is a limited role for some criminal offences. However, the most important backstop that could be provided would be by providing some limited cohabitation rights of the type that exist in neighbouring jurisdictions. The reform proposals presented in the book are designed as a complete package. Focusing on reform of marriage law alone would be insufficient. As argued by Kathy Griffiths, there is a need 'to develop a nuanced approach to reform where both formalised relationships and function-based recognition are used alongside each other in order to create a system that meets the needs of different relationships'.[1]

Given that religions and belief systems invariably have teachings and expectations about family life, a fluid interaction between religion and family law is to be expected. Religious, social, political and legal changes are likely to impact upon one another and have done so for centuries. Although every generation thinks that the challenges they face are unique, calls for marriage reform are by no means a new phenomenon. In the 21st century, however, the need of a modernised law on adult intimate relationships is compelling and, after progressive but ad hoc reforms dealing with same-sex relationships, there is a need to modernise the law on relationships generally as well as to provide limited redress on adult relationship breakdown in relationships where one party has suffered a detriment as a result of the relationship (unless both of the parties have freely and voluntarily opted out). There is a need for a law on adult intimate relationships in England and Wales that reflects the realities of such relationships today.

---

[1] Kathy Griffiths, 'From "Form" to Function and Back Again: A New Conceptual Basis for Developing Frameworks for the Legal Recognition of Adult Relationships' (2019) 31 (3) *Child and Family Law Quarterly* 227, 228.

Index

References to endnotes show both the page number and the note number (231n3).

Lightning Source UK Ltd.
Milton Keynes UK
UKHW020417150222
398707UK00003BB/283